Following nearly two decades of researc... colleagues have brought to light a growi... identify as gay, experience enduring and stable same-sex attractions, and firmly believe that same-sex behavior is morally impermissible. They are highly religious and desire to carry their faith into all aspects of their lives. In this newest work, *Costly Obedience*, a simple question echoes throughout: "Is there a place for these individuals within the church?" The authors answer in the affirmative but point out that the church has not always been well prepared to assimilate these fellow believers. Throughout these pages the reader will learn much about this group, but more importantly he or she will be presented with a challenge that goes beyond merely "accepting" celibate gay Christians into the church community. These believers offer a fresh perspective and model a costly obedience often lacking in today's Western church. This important book will have value not only to pastors and lay leaders but to the church at large, as parishioners seek to create the kind of community that models a costly obedience for all.

Michael Lastoria, professor emeritus, Houghton College, coauthor of *Listening to Sexual Minorities*

In a culture that views sexual activity as a right, the idea of choosing celibacy because another value, namely, one's faith, supersedes that right is unthinkable. Yet celibate gay Christians believe this is what God has called them to do, and they have chosen to obey—despite the cost. Yarhouse and Zaporozhets help us to better understand these Christians, the path they walk, and the sacrifices they make, all for spiritual gain. This willingness to enter into the submission and suffering of Christ for a deeper experience of grace stands in stark contrast to the cheap and easy faith for which too many of us settle. What a beautiful, and hard, testimony this costly obedience is to the church.

Janet B. Dean, associate professor of psychology, Asbury University

Christians almost universally agree that we are called to love our nonheterosexual (LGBTQ+) neighbors. Yet the widespread perception is that we're doing a poor job of it, first and foremost because we do not listen. Informed by first-of-its-kind research among those followers of Christ who often call themselves "celibate gays," this book is essential reading for church and parachurch leaders concerned about the integrity of their ministries and the witness of their congregations and organizations. This book can inform and guide church leaders toward deeper empathy and more effective ministry in a truly marginalized portion of the communities that they serve (and the much larger circle of those who care about them). At a time when the church is on trial before a watching secular world—and often regarded as a bastion of hatred and homophobia—this book offers real solutions and challenges. You will not be disappointed.

Stanton L. Jones, professor of psychology,
Wheaton College

Costly Obedience makes a significant contribution to broader LGB research by considering often neglected aspects of diversity at the intersection of sexuality and religion/spirituality. Sound research on chosen celibacy and/or mixed-orientation marriages is almost nonexistent in the professional literature. This kind of rigorous and reflective study is long overdue! In their scholarship, Yarhouse and Zaporozhets give voice to the lived experience of courageous persons who are negotiating the worlds of faith and same-sex attraction, often caught between a suspicious general culture and an agitated Christian community. In the end, this research narrative speaks to both, calling for deeper understanding of persons who have been largely denied or overlooked. Even more, Yarhouse and Zaporozhets help us understand that we all need to know these colleagues, friends, and family members. Their experience speaks to us.

Stephen P. Stratton, professor of counseling and
pastoral care, Asbury Theological Seminary

COSTLY
OBEDIENCE

COSTLY OBEDIENCE

WHAT WE CAN LEARN FROM THE CELIBATE GAY CHRISTIAN COMMUNITY

MARK YARHOUSE &
OLYA ZAPOROZHETS

ZONDERVAN
REFLECTIVE

ZONDERVAN REFLECTIVE

Costly Obedience
Copyright © 2019 by Mark Yarhouse and Olga Zaporozhets

ISBN 978-0-310-52140-2 (softcover)

ISBN 978-0-310-52142-6 (ebook)

Requests for information should be addressed to:
Zondervan, *3900 Sparks Dr. SE, Grand Rapids, Michigan 49546*

Cover design: Bruce Gore | Gore Studio, Inc.
Cover photo: Tracy Immordino/Alamy Stock Photo
Interior design: Kait Lamphere

Printed in the United States of America

19 20 21 22 23 24 25 /LSC/ 15 14 13 12 11 10 9 8 7 6 5 4 3 2 1

To those whose lives reflect
costly obedience

CONTENTS

FOREWORD

In the summer of 2018, a group of some four hundred Christians gathered in St. Louis, Missouri, for the first annual Revoice conference. On the surface, nothing about Revoice appeared atypical for an event of its kind. A praise band led attendees in singing the latest Christian worship hits. Volunteers dressed in identical T-shirts passed out welcome packets that included a list of breakout sessions and a souvenir handheld fan (it was July in St. Louis, after all). Caterers dished out food at lunchtime to a line that snaked around the perimeter of the basement in the stately old Presbyterian church where the conference was held. In short, to anyone familiar with Christian gatherings, nothing would've seemed noteworthy about Revoice.

This apparent normalcy, though, belied the historic significance of the conference. According to its website, Revoice wanted to "support, encourage, and empower gay, lesbian, same-sex-attracted, and other LGBT Christians so they can flourish while observing the historic, Christian doctrine of marriage and sexuality."[1] For the first time ever, there was now an evangelical Christian organization publicly acknowledging the existence of people who identify as lesbian, gay, or persistently same-sex attracted who nonetheless pledge to live in accord with biblical teaching that sexual intimacy is to be kept within the marriage of a man and a woman. And if the enthusiasm of the attendees was any indication, it had been a long time in coming.

The book you now hold in your hands—a milestone in evangelical Christian publishing, I believe—is intended to introduce you to these gay and lesbian Christians who have committed themselves to biblical faithfulness and help you better understand their unique set of challenges. And, perhaps more importantly, it aims to help their straight counterparts discern and appreciate the gift of their costly witness and the potential it has to bring revival to our churches.

Only a few years ago, a book like this wouldn't have been imaginable. Prior to the early 2000s, most Christians who adhered to traditional biblical interpretation and ethics would have argued that being gay and celibate wasn't an option for faithful Christians. The most prominent ministry to LGBT people in the evangelical world boldly proclaimed, "Change is possible!" implying that same-sex desire could—and should—be left behind through healing prayer, rigorous accountability, and extensive counseling.

But something started to shift as numerous leaders of "ex-gay" ministries began admitting that their promises of change had led to false hope. In 2012, just before the president of the largest Christian organization promoting "freedom from homosexuality" decided to shut down its ministry, he offered a confession of sorts: "The majority of [lesbian and gay] people that I have met, and I would say the majority meaning 99.9% of them, have not experienced a change in their orientation."[2] It was time, in other words, to face the fact that some Christians would experience more or less exclusive same-sex attraction for the duration of their lives.

For some believers, this meant a welcome, newly open door to consider the possibility of permanent same-sex unions or even marriage, which only became legal throughout the US in 2015 and which some churches (mostly mainline Protestant ones) had begun to bless. For other Christians, however, like the ones you'll be learning more about in these pages, acknowledging the permanence of a same-sex sexual orientation didn't involve any shift in Christian moral convictions. These lesbian and gay believers continued to hold to Christianity's historic prohibition of gay sex and began to talk about what it might look like to embrace celibacy and maybe even flourish in it.

Gradually, they began to find their voices. Justin Lee, the founder of the Gay Christian Network (now Q Christian Fellowship), and his Catholic friend Ron Belgau had quietly been paving the way for years. While they didn't see eye to eye with each other about the moral acceptability of same-sex intimacy, they agreed that the "ex-gay" paradigm was untenable and that celibacy should be seen as a viable—even honorable—option for Christians identifying as gay. As Lee would later put it in his 2012 book *Torn: Rescuing the Gospel from the Gays-vs.-Christians Debate*, "Celibacy is an extremely difficult path. It can be lonely and disheartening. Gay Christians who believe this is God's call for them need tremendous support from their church families."[3]

Taking up that same conviction, my book *Washed and Waiting: Reflections on Christian Faithfulness and Homosexuality* told my story of being gay and celibate and discussed my eagerness to see evangelical churches embrace people like me. *Washed and Waiting* was soon followed by Eve Tushnet's *Gay and Catholic: Accepting My Sexuality, Finding Community, Living My Faith*, which sounded many of the same notes, challenging the idea that true intimacy is only available in sexually active partnerships. The Spiritual Friendship blog (spiritualfriendship.org) debuted around the same time, publishing a range of male and female authors who wrote with disarming candor about what it was like to know yourself to be gay or lesbian but also to be committed to celibacy. Many of the writers brainstormed about what sorts of support and encouragement churches could offer people in their shoes. In addition, a private Facebook group sprang up to create an additional network of support for openly gay but theologically conservative Christians. At the time of this writing, planning for the second Revoice conference is underway, and attendance is expected to double.

Not long ago, I sat down for lunch with another celibate gay friend to talk about these massive changes to the Christian landscape in the US. "We really are part of a *movement* now!" she gushed, and I knew exactly what she meant. In the space of only a few years, gay Christians choosing celibacy have emerged from the closet. We're grateful for the freedom we've gained to own up to our sexual orientations, and we're hungry for grace and hope as we commit ourselves to the costly obedience we believe God is asking of us. If you want to get to know us better, to learn how to bless and challenge us as well as how to receive our blessings and challenges in return, there is no better book you could read than this one.

Wesley Hill

PREFACE

J acob was an accomplished director of music at a local church. He had been in this role for more than five years, but it had recently come to the attention of the senior pastor that Jacob identified as gay. Jacob was asked to report to the pastor's office to discuss a blog post he'd recently written, one that used language that had alarmed the pastor. In the blog post, Jacob had described himself as a "celibate gay Christian." The pastor spoke to Jacob about his concerns: "Obviously I don't mind if you live a celibate life. You should refrain from sex until you marry. But calling yourself a 'gay Christian' is like identifying with your sin; do you see that? You unite sin with your Savior in a way that tarnishes the gospel. It also sets a precedent for the rest of the church that sin is okay, that your identity can be in anything you want. That's not going to work around here."

Jacob tried to assure the pastor that calling himself gay was not meant to signal approval of sin. In fact, Jacob was committed to celibacy precisely because he agreed with a traditional Christian sexual ethic. He believed that it was sinful to practice homosexuality, but he also felt that it was necessary to be honest about his journey and his same-sex attraction. Rather than proudly trumpeting his identity as a gay Christian, he had written about how language served many purposes and carefully explained what *it meant for him as a Christian to be more transparent about his same-sex sexuality. Despite his careful and clear explanation, Jacob was let go shortly after the meeting.*

The way Jacob describes himself and understands his own sexuality and faith as a celibate gay Christian has emerged in recent years as an alternative narrative for making sense of one's same-sex sexuality. This book is about people like Jacob who are trying to live with enduring same-sex attractions as followers of Christ.

For several decades, the dominant evangelical Christian response to same-sex sexuality was helping gay people become straight—turning them into "ex-gays." In recent years, ex-gay narratives have been on the decline. What has emerged are alternative narratives. One is a gay-affirming narrative that challenges biblical and theological support for a traditional Christian sexual ethic. Another narrative reflects a traditional Christian sexual ethic but does not take the view that orientation is likely to change or be healed. Some of these Christians are single and describe themselves as celibate gay Christians. Others have entered into what are sometimes referred to as mixed-orientation marriages, which is meant to convey the reality of enduring same-sex sexuality while not calling into question the attractions, closeness, and intimacy a person may have with one's opposite-sex spouse.

One reason for the decline of the ex-gay narrative is the emerging stories of "ex-ex-gays"—people who once claimed to have experienced sexual orientation change but who later recanted. The Christian ministry Exodus once promoted the idea of changing one's homosexual orientation, but it closed its doors in 2013. This closure is viewed by many people as a concrete reflection of the decline of the ex-gay narrative within Christian treatment and ministry. Certainly many Christian ministries still emphasize healing and change as the Christian response to gay orientation. Yet it is impossible to deny that the approach Exodus once took no longer connects with a younger generation of believers today.

What happened? That's an interesting question. Multiple influences contributed to a diminished ex-gay narrative. In terms of changes from a mental health standpoint, in 1973 the American Psychiatric Association voted to remove homosexuality per se from the *Diagnostic and Statistical Manual of Mental Disorders* (DSM). What remained was referred to as ego-dystonic homosexuality, or what we might think of as a mental health concern only if one's sexual orientation was distressing to the person such that they wished to change it. By 1987 the next revision of the DSM removed ego-dystonic homosexuality. Since that time, the major mental health communities have moved away from even the term *homosexuality*, which is viewed as too closely tied to a history of viewing same-sex impulses as a reflection of psychopathology. The linguistic shift is toward terms that reflect identity and personhood (e.g., *gay*) in keeping with related social trends toward greater acceptance and celebration of being gay.

While these changes in mental health classification were taking place, a coalition of ministries would form as Exodus International, which would quickly become the largest umbrella organization for ministries for Christians who wished to change. *Change* in this context could be framed as "leaving homosexuality" or "healing" or "change of orientation," depending on the ministry and preferred language and approach. The language of being "ex-gay" would soon follow. At its peak, Exodus International purported to have about 250 affiliated ministries in North America and additional affiliated ministries in other countries.

While the focus during this time was on the testimonies of ex-gays, we also began to hear stories of ex-ex-gays. These are individuals who stated that they once declared they were ex-gay but later either renounced that or indicated that they weren't being fully honest or that they thought they were at the time but their same-sex sexuality continued to be a part of their experience. Social media created more opportunities for those stories to be shared. Without going into too much detail, several high-profile accounts of leaders in the ex-gay movement called into question the ex-gay narrative.

Exodus International closed in 2013. This closing was controversial to some supporters of such ministries, and many independent ministries would continue to offer similar approaches. Two larger groups, the Restored Hope Network and Hope for Wholeness, have emerged in some minds as the new faces of the ex-gay movement, although neither has had quite the same impact or cultural salience as Exodus.

As the ex-gay narrative diminished in popularity, it was inevitable that a new storyline would arise to take its place. One of the new narratives increasing in popularity today is that of the celibate gay Christian. This group of Christians has been in dialogue with other gay Christians, affirming gay Christians, about matters of faith and sexuality. These dialogues have taken place in different venues, but one group that emerged as especially significant was the Gay Christian Network (GCN) founded by Justin Lee in 2001. GCN hosted annual conferences that featured affirming gay Christians and, perhaps to a lesser extent, celibate gay Christians and was often seen as a unique place for dialogue on matters of faith and sexuality. Some of those who represented a traditional Christian sexual ethic eventually developed a blog, *Spiritual Friendship*, to further the discussions that were important to celibate gay Christians. GCN transitioned into the Q Christian Fellowship in 2017. The vision of Q Christian Fellowship is to "prophetically [model] a world where all LGBTQ+ people are fully loved by family, church, and community, and Christians worldwide live up to their calling to be instruments of grace and defenders of the outcasts."[1] *Spiritual Friendship* sponsored its first conference in 2018 in cooperation with another conference, Revoice, which was interested in "supporting, encouraging, and empowering gay, lesbian, same-sex-attracted, and other LGBT Christians so they can flourish while observing the historic, Christian doctrine of marriage and sexuality."[2]

When celibate gay Christians began speaking into the dialogue in recent years, many people were taken by surprise, including the authors of this book. I suppose we should have anticipated it. Many Christians who experience same-sex attraction have not experienced a change in their sexual orientation, yet they report an ongoing conviction to refrain from same-sex sexual behavior. Such Christians often identify as celibate, though some as we mentioned above may enter into what are referred to as mixed-orientation marriage. Despite their abstinence from same-sex sexual behavior, these individuals are comfortable describing themselves and/or their sexual orientation as "gay." Many regard this language as simply the current vernacular for same-sex sexual orientation.

The emergence of the celibate gay Christian narrative is not without its critics. Many conservative Christians who supported Exodus and related ministries would see a path to healing as the only acceptable one for the follower of Christ. These critics often view "put[ting] to death the misdeeds of the body" (Rom 8:12–13), or sin, as ridding oneself of all ungodly impulses, which is how they conceptualize same-sex attractions. Celibate gay Christians, then, are often viewed with suspicion or worse for failing to put to death sin and for appropriating language from the gay community that critics view as incompatible with an identity in Christ.

This new development—the rise of the celibate gay Christian movement—is growing in popularity and influence, but little research has been done to understand the experiences of same-sex-attracted individuals who decide to remain celibate. To remedy the lack of research and understanding about the movement, we have written this book. Mark Yarhouse has spent two decades conducting research on, and providing therapy services for, Christians who experience a conflict between their same-sex sexuality (or sexual identity) and their faith (or religious identity). Mark is executive director of the Institute for the Study of Sexual Identity at Regent University, where he is the Rosemarie S. Hughes Endowed Chair and Professor of Psychology. Earlier in his career, he collaborated with his mentor, Stanton Jones, to study whether people could change their sexual orientation through involvement in Christian ministries. This early work inspired him to explore the conflict Christians often experience when they do not experience a change in sexual orientation but remain convinced of a historic, biblical sexual ethic. Yarhouse wanted to study sexual identity development and the experiences of Christians who navigate sexual and religious identity conflicts over time. This investigation would lead to several lines of research, including an exploration into the experiences of celibate gay Christians.

Olya Zaporozhets is an associate professor in the School of Psychology and Counseling at Regent University. As director of research for the Institute for the Study of Sexual Identity, Olya has been overseeing two lines of the institute's research, including one on celibate gay Christians that will be discussed throughout this book. The other line of research has to do with the experiences of Christian parents when their children come out to them as LGBTQ+. Zaporozhets is actively engaged with the international community and edited a Russian edition of the text by Yarhouse and Tan titled *Sexuality and Sex Therapy: A Comprehensive Christian Appraisal*. Zaporozhets also facilitated education of Ukrainian clinicians in mental health and sexual therapy skills in response to the pronounced need in wartime when resources are scarce.

We have drawn upon the work of several research projects in writing this book. The central focus of the book is derived from a quantitative study of three hundred celibate gay Christians. We reflect on milestone events in their sexual identity development, emotional well-being, psychological distress, attachment, and religiosity. That study is an extension of an earlier study conducted through the Institute for the Study of Sexual Identity that led to one dissertation and preliminary findings presented at two professional conferences.[3] We are grateful for Christine Baker, who served as the initial project coordinator for this study and completed her dissertation on attachment by analyzing data from 118 celibate gay Christians.

In addition to discussing this large study, we also cite interviews we conducted with thirteen celibate gay Christians and thirteen friends who function as family to celibate gay Christians. These interviews are meant to be illustrative, providing a personal element that complements the data, something that can be lost when simply reading research findings. We also discuss findings from a study of 262 graduates of several Protestant seminaries who serve as pastors in the church today.[4] Some of these findings and interviews were presented at a professional conference[5] or were published in a peer-reviewed journal[6] or as book chapters.[7] Tranese Morgan, Dara Houp, and Julia Sadusky conducted qualitative analysis for the study of celibate gay Christians. Emma Bucher, Justin Sides, and Shane Ferrell each served as project coordinators for the study of pastors' experiences with LGBTQ+ persons. This book also includes additional themes and findings we were unable to include in the published article due to space limitations. Morgan Nicolas served as project coordinator of the friends as family study. Tim Stauffer, Darby Harrell, and Crystal Hamling provided theme analysis of interviews of celibate gay Christians and friends who function as family to celibate gay Christians. We would also like to thank Carson Fuhrman, Joshua Matlack, and Chelsi Creech, who conducted literature reviews to support this book project. In addition, Gregory Coles provided us with copyediting and feedback on an earlier version of the book manuscript.

Several gay Christians also contributed brief essays on some aspect of their experience navigating same-sex sexuality and faith. We want to thank Greg Coles, Bridget Eileen, Jeremy Erickson, and William Summay for their willingness to share their thoughts and experiences.

This book is titled *Costly Obedience* because we want to capture an essential aspect of the experience of celibate gay Christians as they try—however imperfectly—to live a life of chastity today. Our hope is that this information will equip celibate gay Christians, and those who love them, to identify ways to support and encourage one another in the body of Christ. We also hope for a greater expression of empathy and compassion toward celibate gay Christians within the church, as well as greater respect and regard for the decisions made by these individuals. Christians can use this book as an opportunity to reflect on their doctrinal convictions as well as their practice and personal relationships with same-sex-attracted individuals. We hope the church will come to a more nuanced and mutually edifying view of persons who are navigating questions of sexual identity and faith, one that enriches all our relationships and supports a common vision of joy, charity, and Christlikeness.

CHAPTER 1

CHURCH CULTURE ATTITUDES
about LGBTQ+ PERSONS

Stephanie, one of our group members, was in tears. She could not stop sobbing, so the group sat with her in silence for several minutes. Stephanie is a conservative Christian who experiences same-sex attractions, and she was participating in sexual identity group therapy. The focus of the group was to reduce shame among Christians dealing with issues and challenges related to same-sex sexuality. Stephanie had just shared an incident in which a family at her church had asked to be prayed for by "someone else, anyone else" because of the perception that she was a lesbian. Stephanie was hurt, so she spoke to the pastor after the service to relate what had happened. The pastor then spoke with the father of the family and relayed to Stephanie that the father wasn't comfortable being prayed for by Stephanie. Stephanie wept as she told our group that her pastor had sided with the family and had decided not to talk any further with the family about this. Feelings of shame washed over her. We could hear her whispering to herself between her sobs, "What's wrong with me?"

We could share many stories about individuals who identify as gay *and* Christian, individuals who are often "conservative"[1] in other ways as well. Many of these stories are about people trying to live according to a traditional Christian sexual ethic, one in which sex is to be enjoyed within the bounds of marriage between a man and a woman, yet who still experience significant conflicts within their local faith communities.

In this chapter, we begin by considering church culture. Specifically, we want to look at ways in which churches with a traditional Christian sexual ethic may inadvertently create a hostile atmosphere for same-sex-attracted or gay Christians—even those who are committed to the very same sexual ethic as the church and have embraced a commitment to pursue chastity. First, we will look at the wide range of Christian churches that share a traditional Christian sexual ethic and hear from seminary-educated pastors as they describe the atmosphere for discussions of sexuality in these churches. We will conclude by looking at several things we can learn from the experience of celibate gay Christians in these church environments.

WHAT CHURCH?

Data from the Pew Research Center Survey suggests that "acceptance of homosexuality is rising across the broad spectrum of American Christianity," including those who have historically been opposed to same-sex relationships.

> Amid a changing religious landscape that has seen a declining percentage of Americans who identify as Christian, a majority of U.S. Christians (54 percent) now say that homosexuality should be accepted, rather than discouraged, by society. While this is still considerably lower than the shares of religiously unaffiliated people (83 percent) and members of non-Christian faiths (76 percent) who say the same, the Christian figure has increased by 10 percentage points since we conducted a similar study in 2007. It reflects a growing

acceptance of homosexuality among all Americans—from 50 percent to 62 percent—during the same period.[2]

The same study suggests that these changes in attitudes reflect the increasing number of younger voices who tend to be more accepting of same-sex sexuality and sexual behavior:

> Among Christians, this trend is driven partly by younger church members, who are generally <u>more accepting of homosexuality</u> than their elder counterparts. For example, roughly half (51 percent) of evangelical Protestants in the Millennial generation (born between 1981 and 1996) say homosexuality should be accepted by society, compared with a third of evangelical Baby Boomers and a fifth of evangelicals in the Silent generation. Generational differences with similar patterns also are evident among Catholics, mainline Protestants and members of the historically black Protestant tradition.[3]

Despite the growing acceptance of same-sex unions among Christians in the United States, many church denominations as well as many people whose faith traditions clearly teach against same-sex sexual behavior (e.g., Roman Catholics) still adhere to a traditional Christian sexual ethic.

If we want to speak about "the church," we first need to address the question of what church we are referring to. The Christian church is not monolithic but rather encompasses a large number of denominations and traditions with a diversity of doctrines and practices. Any reflection on contemporary church culture will necessarily apply more to some church communities than to others. Our intention in this book, while it may have implications for a broad readership, is to focus more narrowly on the climate and relationships within Christian churches *that adhere to a traditional Christian sexual ethic.* By this we mean the view that sexual behavior is intended to occur exclusively between one man and one woman in the covenantal relationship of marriage.

Both authors of this book come from an evangelical Christian background, and we see our own faith communities struggling to discuss questions about sexual identity and how best to understand lesbian, gay, bisexual, transgender, and queer (LGBTQ+) experiences. So our focus in writing this book is on evangelical Christian churches. One definition of *evangelicalism* describes it as "a fairly discrete network of Protestant Christian movements arising during the eighteenth century in Great Britain and its colonies."[4] However, we need to recognize that the definition of *evangelical* is not fixed, and it can more broadly refer to a category of religious doctrine that transcends denominational and confessional boundaries. We use the term *evangelical* in this broader, more encompassing manner, referring to churches that emphasize the authority of the Bible and the redeeming work of Jesus Christ in the life of the individual, among other components.[5]

Yet even though we focus on evangelical readers as the target audience for this book, we hope to speak to other Christians as well. Many Christians who hold to a traditional Christian sexual ethic would not identify as evangelical, and we hope to count them among our readership. Indeed, we anticipate some readers will be Catholic, some Orthodox, others Protestant,[6] which is very much in keeping with the diversity we have seen in the sample of celibate gay Christians we will discuss throughout this book. As we will see, many of the people we will learn from are practicing Catholic believers. The official teaching of the Roman Catholic Church is that men and women who experience "exclusive or predominant sexual attraction toward persons of the same sex" (§2357) are "called to chastity" (§2358).[7] Roman Catholics are commanded to accept such people "with respect, compassion, and sensitivity" (§2358).[8]

Therefore, the content of this book is focused on addressing Christian churches with a traditional sexual ethic. We are thinking primarily of evangelical Christian churches and other congregations that might not identify as evangelical but who hold to similar doctrinal positions regarding sexual ethics. In doing so, we recognize that we are excluding those churches that have begun blessing same-sex unions. Commonly called "affirming" churches, these churches often identify as mainline or theologically progressive and have chosen to combat the inhospitable church culture by revising their doctrine regarding same-sex relationships. Our intention in this book is not to engage the theological debate that motivates some churches to adopt this "affirming" posture. Instead, we have chosen to address only those churches that adhere to a traditional Christian sexual ethic. We believe that changing one's theology or doctrine is not the only way for churches to grow in compassionate ministry as they engage the topic of sexual identity. If evangelical churches are to grow and develop healthy, compassionate ministry for same-sex-attracted individuals, they must know where they currently stand in relation to sexual minorities. This is where we begin, with the experiences of same-sex-attracted individuals in evangelical churches. What are these evangelical churches like for Christians who experience same-sex attraction?

A Note on Terminology

Before we dive into the details of studies and interviews, we need to define a few terms. Throughout the book, we use terms like *homosexuality*, *same-sex attraction*, *LGBTQ+*, and adjectives like *gay*. *Homosexuality* typically refers to a topic and is rather imprecise for some of the discussions we will be having. A *homosexual orientation* is steady or enduring sexual attraction toward the same sex (in contrast to a *heterosexual orientation*, which refers to steady or enduring attraction to the opposite sex). *Bisexual orientation* refers to attraction to both the same and opposite sex. *Same-sex attraction* refers to sexual attraction toward the same sex. Based on the strength and persistence of that attraction, a person might say that they have a homosexual orientation. However, few people today use the word *homosexual* to describe their orientation. They tend to use the word *gay*. *Gay* can refer then to a person's orientation or can be more of an identity. *Gay* is also an umbrella term that is sometimes used when referencing the lesbian, gay, and bisexual community.

In addition, it is helpful to understand the concept of different "sides" that are used to describe various positions people and churches have taken on the question of how to respond to same-sex attraction. Typically, different letters are used to describe these positions:

> **Side A:** Believe same-sex sexual relationships are morally permissible.
>
> **Side B:** Believe same-sex sexual relationships are not morally permissible.
>
> **Side C:** Are undecided or in tension about whether same-sex relationships are morally permissible.
>
> **Side X:** Believe that same-sex attractions themselves are a moral concern and are attempting to change (or report having changed) their sexual orientation.

This terminology comes from an organization called Bridges Across the Divide.[9] Side A refers to gay Christians who believe that same-sex sexual relationships can be morally permissible, whereas Side B refers to gay Christians who view same-sex sexual relationships as morally impermissible. Side C refers to those who are either undecided or in tension around these conclusions. Bridges developed A, B, and C, and others invented Side X over time as a way of differentiating "gay Christian" side B folks from "ex-gay" side B folks. Those who hold to Side B would not hold out the expectation of changing orientation or attraction, nor hold the belief that it is sin to experience same-sex attractions, whereas Side X tends to view same-sex attractions themselves as a moral concern and are attempting change (or have experienced a change) in their attractions or orientation. Many celibate gay Christians are familiar with this terminology and may use it as shorthand to communicate different perspectives. In our book we are primarily interacting with Christians who identify with Side B, the position that same-sex sexual relationships are morally impermissible.

Environmental Impact on Mental Health

Talking about *how* celibate gay Christians experience church environments is difficult without considering the impact these environments can have on mental health. The prevailing assumption among mental health experts has been that exposure to a non-affirming theology creates stress that places sexual minorities at greater risk for mental health concerns. This assumption is an expression of what is referred to as the "minority stress model." We will spend some time later in the book considering this model in greater detail, but the issues merit at least a brief introduction here.

Minority stress refers to a theory that states that minorities are at greater risk of stress-related health concerns due to their minority status. As gay and lesbian persons are in the numeric minority, they are sometimes referred to as "sexual minorities." The minority stress theory suggests that gay and lesbian persons are at greater risk for health disparities and other mental health concerns related to social stigma.[10]

Barnes and Meyer[11] reported on 355 black, white, and Latino sexual minorities and whether exposure to a traditional Christian sexual ethic (or what the researchers described as "non-affirming religious settings") would lead to increased mental health challenges. Specifically, they measured increases in internalized homophobia (a negative appraisal of one's own same-sex sexuality that is internalized),[12] symptoms of depression, and decreases in well-being. They found that participation in churches that taught a traditional Christian sexual ethic was related to higher levels of internalized homophobia, and that Latinos reported higher internalized homophobia than white sexual minorities:

> While participation in non-affirming religious settings was related to internalized homophobia, and internalized homophobia predicted depressive symptoms and psychological well-being, participation in non-affirming religious settings was not related to adverse mental health outcomes. We suspect that our result is explained, in part, by the countervailing effects of religion among LGB people. One pathway, which we had hypothesized, has negative impact through internalized homophobia, but another pathway leads to a salutary effect through improved social support.[13]

The authors noted that sexual minorities with a faith commitment are about 2.5 times more likely to attend a local religious setting that reflects a Side B theology (or a traditional Christian sexual ethic) than to attend a church that adheres to a Side A theology (or an affirming sexual ethic). In keeping with the minority stress model mentioned above, they see this as increasing the risk of internalized homophobia. However, they recognize that being a part of a religious faith community has benefits (what they call a "salutary effect" of being part of a faith community) that may offset those concerns to some extent.

This study illustrates the complexity of faith experience for celibate gay Christians as diverse and multifactorial. For example, the study indicates that participation in a local faith community, in addition to providing social support, also creates a meaning-making structure for sexual minorities of faith, a means of helping them address questions of purpose, identity, and existence. Having a structure that helps them address questions of ultimate concern for Christians is very compelling, especially when the meaning they find lends itself to unique and edifying contributions to the body of Christ, such as modeling obedience and faithfulness or increasing sensitivity to those who are marginalized.

While this study is helpful in identifying some of the possible mental health concerns and benefits for sexual minorities in traditional faith communities, one of the best ways to understand the culture of these communities and how they understand themselves in light of these questions is to speak with church leaders. What do pastors say about their churches? How do they describe the atmosphere of their church community? Let's turn our attention to the experiences of pastors before examining what celibate gay Christians have to say about their own church experience.

HOW PASTORS DESCRIBE
CHURCH ATMOSPHERE

To better understand the current church atmosphere toward lesbian, gay, bisexual, transgender, queer (LGBTQ+) persons and how these individuals experience the church, we spoke with pastors who have graduated from evangelical seminaries[14] and are currently in the pastorate. We asked them to describe how they perceive the atmosphere or environment of their church in relation to LGBTQ+ persons. Specifically, we asked them to identify which factors they think have directly or indirectly impacted this atmosphere.[15]

Unsurprisingly, many pastors identify their doctrinal teaching as a key factor in creating an atmosphere of potential tension with LGBTQ+ persons. After all, if a church holds to a traditional understanding that marriage is between a man and a woman and that same-sex relationships are morally impermissible, their doctrinal beliefs will inevitably shape church atmosphere in relation to LGBTQ+ persons. One pastor related, "As we definitely view marriage as being between a man and a woman, and as we reinforce such a teaching in the church, then anyone having a same-sex attraction would be continually confronted with this idea and thus feel somewhat uncomfortable." Other church leaders expressed similar views.

The fact that doctrine and teaching on a traditional sexual ethic may lead to tension for LGBTQ+ individuals is not surprising, but it should lead us to additional questions. For example, can a church be "welcoming but not affirming," as many evangelicals say they aspire to be?[16] Can a church hold a traditional Christian sexual ethic but still have an atmosphere that welcomes sexual minorities? Can a church accept same-sex-attracted persons, as the Catholic catechism commands, with "respect, compassion, and sensitivity" (§2358) without altering its doctrine?[17] To answer these questions, we need to explore how well individual congregants interact with beliefs, values, and experiences of sexuality and sexual behavior different from their own.

Sadly, the pastors we spoke with disclosed that some of their church members struggle to interact with alternative worldviews, and this creates a hostile environment for anyone who appears to be an outsider. One pastor explained:

> Our church is made up of people who, while very sincere in their desire to please God and . . . well intentioned in their actions, are closer in comfort with a legalistic viewpoint of Scripture. They genuinely care for outsiders and yet have a hard time understanding and thus accepting someone's view of life and God that is different from their own.

Other pastors were aware of how these attitudes would make it difficult to empathize with people who were navigating same-sex sexuality. For example, one pastor discussed the location of his church and how that location impacted the congregants' capacity for empathy:

We are located in a small town in a largely rural area. Social and religious views are very conservative. People in the area are generally out of touch with issues like same-sex struggles. Those experiencing such struggles no doubt fear making their struggles known because of the rejection and outright attacks they might experience.

Some pastors were also aware of highly intolerant perspectives within their faith communities: "[Gay sexuality] is sort of the unpardonable sin. There can be no such thing as a gay Christian. All of them are going to hell." Needless to say, a church environment where this perspective dominates is unlikely to draw or retain Christians navigating the relationship between their same-sex sexuality and the Christian faith.

A helpful first step in shaping church culture, especially cultures that are hostile or unwelcoming to those with same-sex attraction, is to separate out the *experience* of same-sex attraction from same-sex *behavior*. This simple distinction provides an opening for a person to find support in their church as they try to live a celibate life, which may mean coming to terms with their same-sex attractions as an enduring experience, even while they commit to refraining from sexual behavior. A church's atmosphere and approach to LGBTQ+ experiences should be informed by a combination of *grace* and *truth*. We recognize that this is a delicate balance, more easily stated than achieved, yet in our conversations with pastors we found that it is the balance many churches are striving for. One pastor described his church's approach to LGBTQ+ individuals in precisely these terms: "We are intentional about grace and truth as an approach to dealing with those who have same-sex attraction. We welcome them and share with them as they give us the freedom to do so." Some pastors described how their churches were "in process" in the way they engaged LGBTQ+ experiences. They wanted their churches to be characterized by both grace and truth but felt they hadn't yet fully arrived at this brand of engagement. That is, they were traditional in their sexual ethic but very open to discovering better ways to connect and minister to people navigating sexual identity:

> We are doing better in this regard—our church is starting to become more open about sexual issues, and we have started to help guys and girls deal with them. Dealing in grace and truth with same-sex attraction, however, is the next step and, although we have visited with some people about this issue, I don't yet think people in that position would think our church is a safe place where they will find help and support.

That said, some churches affirm a balance between grace and truth in theory but have no working model of how to put that theory into practice. One pastor commented, "Our congregation is not well schooled in how to maintain a balance between a grace-filled reception of those who have same-sex attraction and yet not presenting themselves as condoning same-sex attraction. Therefore, there is a tendency to avoid and not engage those with same-sex attraction." This comment is indicative of where many evangelical churches are today, especially churches that believe that not only same-sex sexual behavior but also same-sex attraction or orientation is a morally culpable sin. Often these congregations have been strongly influenced by ex-gay narratives and the accompanying theology of the ex-gay movement.

Of course, any evangelical church will likely include a wide and diverse variety of people. Some individuals will be gracious and inviting, while others may give the church a bad name by the way in which they interact with LGBTQ+ persons. One pastor explained how the influence of specific church members can make a church feel hostile—even when the majority of the congregation is welcoming: "There are some members of our church who are intolerant toward homosexuality. To the extent that such intolerance reaches a person with same-sex attraction, they would likely find difficulty here. Most people in our church would be gracious to anyone, regardless of their background (sexual attraction or otherwise)."

This mixed behavior raises a key question for pastors of churches that want to be more welcoming toward those with same-sex attraction. How do you communicate a welcoming atmosphere when some individuals within the church remain negative and intolerant toward those struggling with same-sex attraction? And how do you handle derogatory comments made by individual church members?

Experiences with Derogatory Remarks

Since even churches with a high proportion of welcoming people may still have a few hostile congregants, church climate is inevitably shaped by how churches respond if a church member, staff person, or pastor makes a derogatory remark about people who experience same-sex attraction. We asked the pastors in our study what their experience has been with derogatory comments made by individuals. Some pastors tended to ignore derogatory remarks if they were made offhandedly or were not directly related to the topic of the conversation. For example, one pastor said, "It happened casually in a conversation, as an aside—the focus was not on being derogatory, as the comment was tangential to the topic at hand." Yet even when the derogation played a more central role in conversation, some church leaders admitted that they defaulted to remaining silent. One pastor indicated, "In the context or group that I can remember it happening, nothing was said or done."

Other pastors indicated that they would correct derogatory statements made against sexual minorities. One pastor declared, "I would confront the issue. It is not acceptable in our church to denigrate anyone no matter what their circumstances." Another pastor explained the strategy he would take in correcting whoever made such a statement, a strategy that emphasized their shared humanity: "I would talk with them about the life struggle of those battling same-sex attractions and God's heart and plan for them."

PASTORS' LEVEL OF COMFORT

In many churches holding to a traditional Christian sexual ethic, the church's climate toward LGBTQ+ individuals is heavily influenced by the tone the pastor sets. Congregants who feel unsure of what to believe or how to respond on this topic often mimic the posture of their leaders. This means that a pastor's approach to same-sex sexuality, his experience with the topic, and his level of comfort with gay individuals are important predictors of the overall congregational climate. In our survey of pastors, we asked pastors about their own comfort level with individuals who experience same-sex attraction or identify as gay.[18] We received a wide range of responses, as one might imagine. Some pastors were quite comfortable, while others admitted to significant discomfort, and we saw everything in between these two extremes.

Among pastors who said they were comfortable discussing same-sex sexuality and interacting with gay-identifying or same-sex-attracted people, many had been influenced by personal encounters or experiences with LGBTQ+ individuals in the past. Pastors who reported a higher degree of comfort often shared how they had friends or family members who identified as gay and how these relationships provided them an opportunity to become more comfortable discussing same-sex sexuality, which they otherwise might not have experienced. For example, one pastor spoke of his relationship with his son who is gay: "We have gone from no contact, to contact with our son only, to contact with our son and his gay partner. Everyone in our extended family has their own personal tolerance level. I pray consistently that our son would overcome his sexual orientation and that his partner would come to know the Lord."

While this comment reflects a positive and optimistic willingness for further engagement, we should caution that this journey is probably still ongoing, and the pastor's experience with one gay family member doesn't mean that he is now automatically at ease with all LGBTQ+ people and interactions. The point is that his personal relationship with his son has provided him numerous opportunities to become more comfortable around people who are traversing this terrain.

On the other side, we are concerned that this pastor's language about everyone having "their own personal tolerance level" indirectly communicates an attitude that gay people are a dangerous substance that one must be careful exposing oneself to. We believe that this caution, while understandable, is not the best starting point for establishing relationships. The use of language like "overcome his sexual orientation" could indicate a hope that the son experiences conviction about sexual practice and refrains from same-sex behavior. More likely, statements like this express a goal or desire to see a person shift from gay to straight or a hope that the individual will no longer experience same-sex attraction. Again, while the context of personal relationships can be instructive, the assumptions that lie behind these personal interactions may also lead to problems in pastoral care or develop a church climate that negatively impacts the experiences of those who choose to pursue celibacy. Church culture will be shaped by this pastor's assumption that the desired and ideal outcome for gay Christians is to shift to a heterosexual orientation, what is sometimes referred to as healing from homosexuality. While this attitude is understandable, it may set up unrealistic expectations for change that could result in greater shame for those who do not experience change, while failing to provide adequate support to those whose same-sex sexuality is an ongoing experience.[19]

Another pastor related, "My brother-in-law is a very active homosexual, and he is very involved with me and my family. This typically means he and his partner, as well as [their] social circle are welcomed into our home, or we will spend recreational/social time with them." While not every pastor who felt comfortable around sexual minorities had an experience like this one, we did see that having some kind of personal contact tended to increase people's comfort levels with the LGBTQ+ community. Growing in comfort with sexual minorities is itself a process, but it is important for church leaders who want their churches to be welcoming for sexual minorities to consider how they personally, as well as members of their congregations, can begin to grow in this area.

Other pastors identified themselves as "in process" in developing their personal comfort level. They may have begun a journey toward increased comfort in this area, but they were conscious that they hadn't yet arrived at the level of comfort they hoped to achieve in the future. These pastors may have had relationships with LGBTQ+ persons, but they didn't report the same level of peace in these relationships as did those pastors who were more comfortable with the LGBTQ+ population. One pastor spoke to their experience by saying, "I have friends from college who are homosexual or have dealt with same-sex attraction. I know individuals outside of my church—teachers, for instance—who are homosexual. So I have some interaction. I am not 'very comfortable' but I am not uncomfortable either when it comes to interacting with them."

Some of our pastors acknowledged that their conservative Christian subculture communicates the message that Christians should stay away from the LGBTQ+ community. One pastor commented, "I have a large amount of experience with being surrounded by people with same-sex attraction and/or identity. Familiarity has granted me an ability to be quite comfortable with a group of people my culture had told me to isolate." For this pastor, personal experience became a strategy for overcoming the dominant attitudes of his Christian subculture. Other pastors shared how education and training helped equip them. One pastor, for example, said, "Taking the Human Sexuality class at [a seminary] and counseling several people over the years, I have become very aware of the need that exists and enjoy ministering to those individuals."

In addition to discussing personal contact, education, and training, some pastors mentioned how the cross of Christ highlights our common need, leveling all of humanity, both gay and straight. The recognition that we are all incomplete, sinners in need of a savior, made these pastors more comfortable in their interactions with LGBTQ+ individuals. On this point, one pastor commented: "My convictions about the gospel are that they don't affect my view of a person with any sort of addiction or propensity to any particular sin. As a Christian I am no less needy of God's grace today than I was the day before I became a Christian. This helps me see anyone else, with same-sex attraction or not, as a sinner needy of God's grace just like me."

However, how LGBTQ+ persons approached their own sexuality was important to some pastors. Were they currently engaging in same-sex sexual expression? If so, were these individuals "sincere strugglers," or were they "assertive advocates" of their right to sexual expression?[20] The answers to these questions were determinative for how pastors chose to engage with sexual minorities. For example, one pastor acknowledged:

> It really depends on the person. Since I believe Scripture teaches that a lifestyle of such behavior (along with adultery, fornication, and thievery) is not consistent with being a believer, I would be cautious around those who claimed Christ and felt no conviction or desire to change from their behavior. On the other hand, someone acknowledging their behavior

as sin, but still struggling in the grip of that sin, I would be very comfortable with.

Still other pastors found that their discomfort was rooted in a lack of understanding, either because they were uncertain how to respond or because they had difficulty empathizing with sexual minorities. One pastor didn't feel uncomfortable interacting with LGBT people in general but felt great discomfort not knowing how to counsel LGBTQ+ persons well: "I am comfortable discussing virtually any issue that someone may be struggling with. But I am not very confrontational, which makes me feel a little tentative . . . torn between feeling that I should say something but not doing so." Another pastor's discomfort was rooted in a lack of understanding of the sexual minority experience: "I don't understand what it feels like to experience SSA [same-sex attraction]. I admit that I'm fully baffled by how a man could be sexually attracted to a man. I can get past it, but I'd be lying if I said that I wasn't at least a little uncomfortable."

One way pastors seemed to counteract feelings of "difference" between themselves and sexual minorities was to underscore their "similarities." Often, the similarity they emphasized was their common experience of the fall and the corresponding struggle with sin. For example, one pastor said, "Same-sex attraction is a struggle just as my own sin is a struggle. I have the hope and answer to their problem, but if I condemn them, I lose the right to share the real answer that is Jesus! Speak truth covered in love and respect, but speak truth, not enablement." Another pastor put it this way: "All people need is Christ. Regardless of the sin, I find generally positive responses to sharing the truth of the gospel with everyone. It is never so much about the sin(s) as it is the Savior. Sin must be honestly spoken of, but the point is to confess a sinful nature more than a particular sin. A nature that can be changed with Christ." Yet another pastor shared, "We are among sinners wherever we go.

God loves sinners and died for them. Acknowledgment of our sin is a necessary step to calling on God to save and seeking a Savior. Anyone, however, who firmly resists that homosexuality (or you name the sin) is wrong in God's sight will be less comfortable around those who believe otherwise, and vice versa."

Each of these quotes illustrates a common theme of viewing sin in the person who experiences same-sex attraction and finding ways to be honest about that sin as a way to direct people toward their need of a savior. However, one problem we noted with these responses was a lack of precision and nuance in a pastoral care response and in the establishment of a welcoming church climate. For example, if by "homosexuality" the pastor quoted above means sexual practice, that means something different than if he is using "homosexuality" to refer to same-sex attraction or a homosexual orientation. The most optimistic interpretation we can take of pastors who encouraged same-sex-attracted people in their churches was that these individuals should let their sinfulness (which they invariably have, like everybody else) drive them toward Jesus. We are concerned about the implications for same-sex-attracted individuals when pastors have the assumption that attraction or orientation is itself sinful. In our experience, such a view can lead to unrealistic expectations for change and a limited view of what constitutes healing and sanctification in the life of the person who experiences same-sex attraction.

Other pastors we spoke with reframed the topic to focus more clearly on how both they and LGBTQ+ persons are called to grow in Christlikeness. For example, one pastor said, "I realize [the LGBTQ+ discussion] has moved for me from less comfortable to more comfortable as we seek to be like Christ with them." Some pastors had a history of conflict with the LGBTQ+ community that impacted their level of comfort with conversations about sexuality. One pastor felt as if "any response short of condoning same-sex activity is viewed as intolerant and bigoted," while others had experienced "belligerent" interactions with members of the LGBTQ+ community. Another pastor disclosed, "As long as I'm not treated with hostility, or exposed to what I might label 'in your face' public displays of affection (which would make me uncomfortable in the case of heterosexual couples too), I am comfortable around people who experience same-sex attraction." Or consider this pastor's experiences with visitors to his church: "People that we have met as visitors to our church who are experiencing same-sex attraction are most often defensive and ready to make assumptions about our reaction, based on very stereotypically described responses from churches." A number of reports like this one speak to the unfortunate reality of conflicted interactions between pastors and members of the gay community.

Some pastors understood that many members of the gay community had already had fairly negative experiences with Christians. They felt some of the anger and injury from those exchanges and the apparent guardedness of some LGBTQ+ persons toward any type of ministry relationship: "I love the opportunity to befriend and bridge the gap with someone who has been hurt by the church or turned away. I see it as an opportunity to demonstrate a full measure of grace and truth." Some pastors spoke of creating an atmosphere of greater transparency for everyone. Such an atmosphere may take years of faithful investment before its fruit becomes apparent. For example, one pastor related:

> Over the years in men's discipleship groups (typically while or after sharing life maps), I've had several men want to visit and discuss sexual struggles—including same-sex attraction. Although I haven't experienced the same personally, I do not find it difficult to resonate with them in the struggles of the flesh. They end up appreciating the safety of a conversation where they can be completely honest and not feel rejected or feel the need to defend or persuade to another position.

So far we have noted that culture and climate are shaped not only by a church's doctrine of sexual ethics but also by whether pastors know and interact with members of the gay community. We have heard pastors discuss their own experiences and comfort levels interacting with people who are same-sex attracted or identify as gay. Additionally, we recognize that these pastors are not a representative sample of all Christian leaders in Protestant or Catholic traditions. But it is still instructive to hear directly from seminary-educated pastors about their experiences with sexual identity and the LGBTQ+ community. Their comments help us identify some of the challenges the church faces today in dealing with sexual identity.

Of course, while pastors can provide some help in understanding the challenges sexual minorities face in evangelical churches that hold to a traditional sexual ethic, the pastoral view is necessarily a partial one. To deepen our understanding of the complexity of this conversation, we have sought out the experiences of celibate gay Christians themselves. What experiences have celibate gay Christians had with the church, and what can these experiences teach us about church culture?

WHAT DO CELIBATE GAY CHRISTIANS SAY?

The Institute for the Study of Sexual Identity has completed several studies of celibate gay Christians. In one smaller study, we asked celibate gay Christians about their experiences in the church.[21] Here, in brief, is a summary of what they shared with us.

Church Talk

According to some of the celibate gay Christians we surveyed, their churches do not address sexuality at all, let alone issues related to sexual identity. A thirty-nine-year-old respondent shared, "Homosexuality was hardly ever mentioned by the leaders of the church." We have found similar results from our interviews of sexual minorities at Christian colleges and universities around the US.[22] Others we spoke with believed that some churches were beginning to wade into the conversation on sexuality and sexual identity, but they felt that these late entries were poorly timed and ineffective. For example, Geoff, a twenty-four-year-old Caucasian celibate man, shared his observations: "So churches are starting to have conversations about homosexuality or same-sex attraction, but I feel that a lot of it is almost like too little, too late."

Several respondents to our survey felt that sexual concerns, when they were mentioned, were not treated equally. Understanding and grace were extended toward individuals with a variety of sexual challenges, yet sexual identity concerns (related to homosexuality) were given little, if any, grace: "There was a huge dissonance between language they used for some sexual struggles that most people were going through and the language used for homosexuality. So when I realized I was attracted to other guys, my reaction was basically to be very frustrated with that hypocrisy and to think that they ought to apply . . . that same sort of grace to my situation."

Others sensed an atmosphere of fear about even speaking of the topic of sexuality in churches. A younger interviewee from a mixed-race background commented, "In more conservative circles of Christianity, there is a fear of the *g*-word [*gay*]." Many people we interviewed were raised in a Christian church that taught that same-sex behavior was morally impermissible. One person, whom we will refer to as Charles,[23] said, "I became a Christian when I was about the age of seventeen, so I kind of understood from early on that the Christian walk did not go along with actually acting out in a same-sex relationship." Similarly, Ben, a younger celibate gay Christian, shared,

I have experienced same-sex attraction from a very early age, pretty much as long as I can remember . . . as early as six

or five years old, and it's amazing to me how I was able to
pick up on how my attractions were unacceptable. . . . Yet I
picked up on these completely unarticulated social cues that
this was not normal or acceptable, so from a very early age
I kept it under wraps.

Ben later told us, "When I first came out, I understood that the
church taught that same-sex relations were not normal, so since
that point it's been a journey of finding out why that is." Jean,
a twenty-eight-year-old Caucasian female, said,

I grew up in the church. My dad was a pastor when I was a
kid. I never really questioned my faith, yet I felt that, from an
appropriate age at least, it was my own—not just my family's
or my parents' faith. But, to me, I guess it's something that
I've always understood about—a marriage is between a man
and a woman. I don't see any evidence otherwise in the Bible.

The Question of Salvation

There were times, however, when the message about what
was morally impermissible was directly tied to the question of an
individual's salvation. As Jean commented,

That's my biggest problem. It's when people put . . . something about homosexuality up there with a salvation issue.
If you're gay, you're not Christian, or, even if you're not acting or behaving or engaging in behavior with somebody of
the same sex . . . it's a lot of times equated with "you're not
a Christian" or somehow a salvation issue, and I have a big
problem with that.

Similarly, Desmond, a twenty-seven-year-old Caucasian,
said, "I was raised with the traditional view that same-sex sexual

activity was wrong. Originally I was raised in the Side X or ex-gay context—that was the context that was sort of the expected response to homosexuality as a Christian. And I spent a few years in ex-gay therapy." As a reminder, the language of being "Side X," or what this interviewee described as "ex-gay," reflects the view that gay Christians should change their sexual orientation and become straight—or at least that they should cease being gay.

The Expectation of Change

Understanding how celibate gay Christians experience the expectation that a Christian *ought* to be Side X, and how this expectation informs the broader church climate, is important. Some of the celibate gay Christians we spoke with talked about their exposure to a Side X message in the church—that is, the expectation that they must change their sexual orientation to be faithful followers of Christ. One interviewee, Xavier, age thirty-two, shared about his experiences with a popular ex-gay ministry. He reflected on his experiences with the leader of that ministry:

> I've seen enough [of ex-gay ministry] to be hesitant at best and against it at worst. The interactions I had with [one ministry leader] seemed to be . . . , in some instances, your relationship to Jesus hinged on how attracted you felt to men in a given moment. While that's probably not a fair catego-rization, there were things I picked up along the way, sort of an ethos there that seemed to be to his logical conclusion. I would say in summary I'm pretty against it.

Charles also shared his views about the attempt to change same-sex attractions or orientation, often referred to as repara-tive therapy. Reparative therapy is a therapeutic approach based on the assumption that our sexual desires are shaped by unmet emotional needs in relation to an individual's same-gender parent:

"The reparative side never felt like it made sense with my experience. . . . I couldn't understand how God would transform someone, or it seemed like a much more remote thing than they would describe."

Desmond described his experience with a Christian ministry in the Catholic tradition named Courage that focuses on the transformational change associated with growing deeper in faith. He pointed out that the language they use in that ministry could be an obstacle to making a person feel comfortable enough to stay with the group. He added that he is not interested in groups that do not reflect a traditional Christian sexual ethic, but disclosed several concerns about this ministry:

> I'm glad Courage exists, but I am not especially eager to touch it with a ten-foot pole. . . . I am not interested, personally, probably because they're extremely hostile to using any type of LGBT language, identifying as gay, etc., but I do that, so I don't think I would feel welcome. . . . Having a gay lifestyle and being sexually addicted are not [synonymous], but that's pretty much the only paradigm Courage has for ex-gay people. . . . At any rate, for people who do find it helpful, I am delighted that it's there, but I can't really see myself getting much out of it. There just aren't a lot of other options, or if there are I don't know about them. There are other Catholic societies, but a lot of them are theologically questionable. That's just something I don't have a lot of interest in.

Another interviewee, Jean, described the message she hears in her church as saying that she is the one who needs to be "fixed," even more so than those facing issues like divorce:

> In a way, it manages to obsess them and makes everything all about you all the time. You know, always makes me the

broken one, I'm the one that needs fixing if I'm the one struggling with this. I can't love other people, I can't offer them anything, or I certainly can't serve them in church or care for other people that might be struggling with divorce or a child abusing drugs or simply depression, and there's just kind of this mentality that keeps—it's like keeping a person on crutches to say that this isn't healed—this broken leg of yours isn't healed until you're straight.

As we alluded to earlier, one of the most significant developments in ex-gay ministry in recent years has been the closure of Exodus International. For decades, Exodus International was the flagship evangelical ministry for people struggling with homosexuality. Affiliated Exodus ministries would offer experiences that included prayer, Bible reading, accountability, and a variety of reading materials. Exodus was widely viewed by critics, fairly or not, as promising an outcome it could not deliver—namely, a complete change of sexual orientation from gay to straight.

Exodus closed in 2013.[24] The controversial closing of Exodus was celebrated by many LGBTQ+ people who felt that Exodus's efforts to change one's sexuality were not helpful and were frequently harmful to those who attended. Some evangelicals who had been involved in Exodus affiliates regrouped and began other ministries. How did celibate gay Christians respond to the closing? This event certainly had an impact, as many of our interviewees mentioned it in their interviews, even when we did not ask about it. Some of those interviewed had been part of an Exodus-affiliated ministry or had otherwise attempted to change from gay to straight. Others told us that they had never felt that becoming heterosexual was a goal they wished to pursue, so they had not been involved with Exodus. Still others expressed ambivalence about the closing of this flagship ministry because of what it represented—an umbrella organization that provided a point of connection with other gay

Christians in the evangelical church. For example, Aiden, a twenty-eight-year-old Caucasian male and celibate gay Christian, shared the following: "I've been thankful that Exodus has ended now, but I kind of long for something in the absence of that. There is a vacuum left, as far as a kind of a national network there."

VACUUM OR VOCATION?
Anonymous

I believe there are only two possibilities for gay people in the church. Either there is a universal cure for homosexuality and by God's grace, all can be made straight, or there must be another vocation open to those for whom marriage is unrealistic or inadvisable.

The ex-gay movement failed because heterosexual marriage was put forward as the universal gold standard to which all people with same-sex attraction were called. Many of these marriages proved to be disastrous, and spouses and children were often deeply hurt as a result. The error in this approach lay in failing to consider the alternative to heterosexual marriage: *celibacy*. Some will argue that ex-gay groups did consider celibacy as a possibility, but typically, if a person was capable of being chaste, that was not seen as *good enough*. Many of my celibate friends, those who later left the "ex-gay" world, were told (and some continue to be told) that they should hope and pray for marriage. If an individual came to see heterosexual marriage as unlikely, this represented a lack of faith on their part.

This way of thinking puts people in a very difficult position. If you're told to see celibacy as a kind of antechamber where you sit patiently, having faith that God will make you straight, then your entire life becomes a process of waiting for something that may or may not happen. Celibacy, understood in this way, is not a vocation—a calling—so much as a vacuum.

This is not how celibacy is presented in the New Testament. In the New Testament, it was Christ who first gave us a hint as to the purpose of the celibate life. He referred to "those who choose to live like eunuchs for the sake of the kingdom of heaven" (Matt 19:12). The apostle Paul expanded on this idea, permitting marriage and suggesting that celibacy is actually a higher calling:

> An unmarried man is concerned about the Lord's affairs—how he can please the Lord. But a married man is concerned about the affairs of this world—how he can please his wife—and his interests are divided. An unmarried woman or virgin is concerned about the Lord's affairs: Her aim is to be devoted to the Lord in both body and spirit. But a married woman is concerned about the affairs of this world—how she can please her husband. I am saying this for your own good, not to restrict you, but that you may live in a right way in undivided devotion to the Lord. (1 Cor 7:32–35)

In this view, celibacy is not a state of waiting, hoping, and praying for marriage. Its purpose is not the rejection of sex or the maintenance of one's purity but an "undivided devotion to the Lord." Paul's singleness freed him to traverse the ancient world, spreading the gospel without fear that he would leave behind a widow and orphans. Perpetual, intentional singleness is not only a possibility for the Christian but is the way of life practiced both by our Lord and by Paul. Both men embraced celibacy for the kingdom, freeing themselves full-time to preach the gospel and build up the church.

This is where many gay Christians run into problems today in their churches. Churches may be happy to advocate celibacy for their LGB parishioners, but they are reluctant to view that celibacy as a gift. Gay and lesbian Christians are often excluded from ministry and remain on the margins of parish life, even if they accept the traditional biblical teaching on sexuality. They are commanded to adopt a state of life whose purpose is service to the body of Christ, then held at arm's length. This makes it difficult for them to serve and honor their calling.

When churches embrace LGB people, inviting them fully into the life of the parish, they enable and support the call to celibacy. A single person's life is no longer just an endless process of saying no to sexual urges and desires for companionship. Instead, it becomes an invitation to join in the rich family life of the church. And, of course, the church in return is enriched by the work that celibate men and women are freed to do for the sake of the kingdom.

Guilt by Association?

Some celibate gay Christians felt overlooked or ignored in the discussion about same-sex sexuality. They mentioned that they were associated with those who held different views and not given consideration for the conservative beliefs they faithfully held and practiced. Aiden related: "I would kind of get thrown in with the liberal, gay image that was kind of out there, and . . . be associated with that and not actually taken for me being me."

In addition, some felt that their churches saw them as a topic to be debated. In response, they said they were tempted to retreat into a posture of self-defense. Many mentioned that in adopting this defensive posture they had few places to turn and were caught between two opposing sides. Given their conservative beliefs, they were unable to find much support *outside* of the church. Geoff, a twenty-four-year-old celibate gay Christian, shared:

> There are times that I still could very well get fed up with the whole overall church and all of that, like with my constant need to defend myself in all directions. You know, it goes to the whole culture being really far away from where I'm at and the way that they teach and preach it. But . . . I won't really have a place in the broader culture. I'll just be this weird, constantly self-hating person.

Noel, a twenty-eight-year-old celibate gay Christian shared a similar feeling of being out of place in both the secular culture and his conservative church:

> It's a unique experience: you're way too conservative and not living into who you're supposed to be for Side A Christians generally, and certainly the broader gay culture, but also the straight ally culture that's so much picked up in gay culture. And then for the conservative churches, you're still too far out there; the minute you identify as gay, you're already put in a separate league from the people that are straight.

No Discussion of What Gay Christians Should Do

A majority of the celibate Christians we talked with shared a longing for nurture from the church and further direction and guidance, more than just a list of prohibitions. Eve Tushnet has written that gay Christians cannot have a vocation of "no."[25] By this she means that the church often emphasizes what gay Christians cannot do or cannot have—things like marriage, sexual intimacy, and so on. What gay Christians need from the church is a positive vision for how to faithfully live their lives and serve God. Several of our interviewees spoke specifically about this, how the church emphasizes what gay Christians *cannot* do while offering little help in understanding what they *can* do. For example, Eugene, a twenty-four-year-old Korean-American celibate man, said, "Somebody asked a good question—the Christian community, they always tell us not to do something. Not to be in relationships, not to engage in sexual impurity or whatever, but we never really talk about what we should do with our sexuality. So I'm in search of what God is calling us to do, not what not to do."

This remains an unanswered question that the church will need to address if it wishes to welcome gay Christians committed to chastity. For Christians who refrain from same-sex behavior, is there a path toward meaning and purpose, a way of contributing to the body of Christ and to society that can be explored and discussed more openly? This question is one we will return to later.

A Sacramental Understanding

We also heard from a subset of Catholic interviewees who had found in their Catholicism some additional resources to aid them in their pursuit of celibacy. These interviewees spoke about the role of the sacraments in their tradition and the depth of teaching on historical models of celibacy in the Catholic tradition. These are features of Catholicism that are foreign to most Protestant traditions, where celibacy may be seen as an incomplete goal falling short of marriage, an undesirable state. Catholicism has typically associated a call to celibacy with a higher order of ministry and vocation, such as the priesthood, and the honor and dignity the tradition provides to this vocation may resonate better with some celibate gay Christians. For example, Liam, a twenty-four-year-old

Caucasian celibate gay Christian, shared about the role of the Catholic practice of confession in his life: "Again, [the welcome I received from my priest] was just something that came out in the context of confession; we didn't really have a discussion about it generally. I just knew that if I needed to I could talk to him about it."

Alex, an eighteen-year-old biracial celibate gay Christian, told us about the place of the sacraments in his life: "I think the thing that helps the most on my faith journey is the sacraments. As a Catholic, I have a very strong sense of sacramental faith that God uses ordinary things and uses them supernaturally." He later added, "Catholicism has a much deeper position on celibacy, and in that there's a distinct celibate voice within Catholicism."

Perhaps one of the lessons here is that Protestants should be willing to listen and learn from Catholic churches, particularly with regard to the respect they have for the vocation of celibacy and how this calling is lived out in a broader church community. The question of how celibacy fits into the Protestant church tradition is particularly relevant as these churches learn how to minister to brothers and sisters who experience same-sex attractions.

A Note on Positive Experiences

Although most of the church experiences related by celibate gay Christians in our survey were challenging or negative experiences, in some instances—like the above-mentioned reference to the sacraments—a celibate gay Christian spoke of a positive experience within the church. Charles had several positive things to say about his church engagement:

> I was involved in an amazing church that . . . is still a great role model for a church that welcomes and creates a really rich space for same-sex-attracted believers but also holds to orthodox Christian theology on sexuality. I was also encouraged from the very beginning to be honest about my shame,

or anything, from any of my pastors. And I felt no pressures to really change orientation, or to do anything other than to follow as a single person. And so, I think I began to get a deeper understanding of Reformed theology and of the role of the church, and of how it was God's plan for all humans to be in a rich relationship within the context of the church, and to really live out our lives in relationship to Christ's church on earth.

We will say more about *what* a church can do to be more supportive of celibate gay Christians in chapter 5. For now, we simply want to give readers a taste of the challenges sexual minorities can face in their faith communities and a hint that there are many gifts they can experience in these communities as well.

For many people outside the church, the idea that gay Christians might have positive experiences in the church is hard to accept. In a recent study on sexual minorities at Christian colleges and universities, we reported that while there are microaggressions against sexual minorities, there are also micro-*affirmations*: moments, gestures, and relationships that helped the person know they were seen and valued in their community.[26] This is something we need to remember—not all experiences are negative or harmful.

However, the negative experiences many gay celibate Christians have had in the church do have a cumulative effect, especially when experienced in contrast to the message of the broader culture. Keep in mind that sexual minorities are not raised in a Christian vacuum, entirely separate from the broader society and the events happening in Western culture. They are raised in a broader cultural context that is now remarkably affirming of same-sex attraction and behavior, one that offers a stark contrast to some of the condemnation they may have heard or experienced in their own churches. This information can provide church leaders with some insight into how to respond to those who experience same-sex attraction, especially as it relates to the development of a welcoming culture in the church.

LANGUAGE AND CHURCH CULTURE

One key factor in the creation of church culture is the church's preferred terminology—the words, phrases, and terms used to describe something. Many churches with a traditional sex ethic prefer descriptive language in discussions on the topic of sexuality. In our experience, such churches tend to avoid or reject sexual identity labels such as *gay*, *lesbian*, or *queer*, often treating such labels as incompatible with a Christian identity. They tend to discourage people who experience same-sex attraction from the use of such self-defining attributions. Rather than saying, "I am gay," a person might be encouraged to say, "I am a Christian who experiences same-sex attraction."

Several years ago, Mark was speaking at a conservative youth ministry conference with a celibate gay Christian friend who had been in ministry to LGBTQ+ youth for many years. A woman neither of them knew came up to Mark's friend and asked her directly, "Why do you insist on identifying with your sin?" This is a common perspective. For some Christians, the terms *gay* and *Christian* are perceived to be incompatible. They represent two opposing moral visions that cannot be brought together in any meaningful or coherent way.

Language matters. The words and terms we use communicate what we believe and will frame the boundaries of any discussion. As a starting point, we have found it helpful to ask celibate gay Christians what different terms mean to them. We will discuss their answers to this question in later chapters, but here we want to raise the point that language influences church culture, which in turn shapes that church's climate for sexual minorities. It is within a linguistically inflected environment that people develop their sense of identity as they navigate questions of sexuality and faith and the intersection between these two important aspects of their personhood.

As we consider the perspectives of evangelical pastors and listen to voices of celibate gay Christians as they speak about evangelical church culture, it is helpful to close this chapter by reflecting on what the evangelical Christian church and celibate gay Christians share in common, as well as some of the areas where they may be speaking past one another. We should not forget or minimize the unity we share as believers through our relationship with Christ. This unity is always of foremost importance in these discussions. In addition, there is a shared sexual ethic, one in which same-sex sexual behavior is viewed as morally impermissible. We should not forget that we are discussing gay Christians who are trying to live a life of celibacy in response to church teachings affirmed by church leadership.

Despite these commonalities, there are at least two facets of the conversation where we see church leaders and celibate gay Christians speaking past one another. Both of them are related to *expectations of change*. These expectations of change are partially rooted in theological beliefs about the inherent sinfulness of the same-sex-attracted state. While not all pastors with a traditional sexual ethic hold this view, a good number seem to hold to the understanding that being same-sex attracted is inherently sinful. A second and related concern is the imprecise language often used in these discussions. When a pastor responds to an LGBTQ+ person by saying, "All they need is Christ," the applications of that statement for everyday life aren't immediately clear. Most celibate gay Christians would heartily agree that they need Christ. But what does this mean when they have Christ? Does this mean they should become straight? Should they be healed? Does that healing mean becoming heterosexual? Would pastors expect same-sex attraction to abate? These are all questions that need to be discussed. On the other hand, it is worthwhile for pastors and those with same-sex attraction to consider if there might be spiritual benefits to how a person responds to an enduring reality, as is often the case with same-sex sexuality. The questions we hear from both pastors and celibate gay Christians are often similar, even if they arise from different contexts and experiences. Pastors are trying to find words and ways to care for people with same-sex attractions in their churches, and celibate gay Christians are longing for nurture and mentoring from their spiritual leaders and guides.

We suggest that conversations about the language we use provide an excellent starting point in addressing these questions. Pastors and celibate gay Christians can work together to agree on language and defining terms, and this seems to be an important factor in making a person with same-sex attractions feel welcomed in the community. For example, what does it mean when gay Christians refer to themselves as "gay"? What concerns would pastors have about using this terminology? Why might language matter to the gay Christian? These are all great questions, and our research leads us to believe these are areas where people may be speaking past one another.

CONCLUSION

In this chapter, we have begun thinking about the culture of the church and how it addresses and shapes our understanding of sexual identity. We invite readers to reflect on their own local church culture and how that culture might be perceived and experienced by others, especially those who are same-sex attracted. What are some of the messages a sexual minority might hear in your church? What overt statements, perhaps about what is morally permissible and morally impermissible, would they hear? Are there subtler messages about marriage or heterosexuality that are a part of your faith community? Does your church culture tend to normalize some problems over others? For example, are other issues like divorce or premarital sex seen as a lesser problem or given less attention than same-sex attraction? And how much of this messaging is intentional, and how much is an unintentional result of the way things are done? How does your church handle the language it uses in communicating and discussing same-sex attraction? Finally, what are your own thoughts about language? How might two different people view decisions about language differently? And what is your church's approach to mentoring members to a strong walk with Christ and Christian living, especially in challenging times? These are all wonderful questions to begin considering, and in the chapters to come we hope to provide some additional guidance and direction as we listen to the voices of celibate gay Christians and learn from their experiences.

FOR DISCUSSION

1. How would you describe your own church climate with respect to discussing sex and sexuality in general and, specifically, LGBTQ+ experiences?
2. What are some of the overt and subtler messages about sexuality and LGBTQ+ issues that might be part of your faith community?
3. How much of your church climate is intentional and how much is unintentional?
4. How does your faith community respond to language? What are your own thoughts about language? How might two different people view decisions about language differently?
5. What are the ways that your church provides nurture and care to its members to help them grow and overcome life challenges?

CHAPTER 2

LGBTQ+ CULTURE
and the CHURCH

I think the gay community, just like anybody,
should be represented in all forms and all types.

Cameron Monaghan

I believe we all have different ways we came to
the gay community and we can't and shouldn't
be pigeonholed into one cultural narrative which
can be [noninclusive] and disempowering.

Cynthia Nixon

In this chapter, we want to take a closer look at the lesbian,
gay, bisexual, transgender, and queer (LGBTQ+) community.
At the outset, it is important to make the same point we made in
our earlier reference to the Christian church—there is no single,
representative way to describe gay culture. Instead, what we find
is a remarkable diversity within the LGBTQ+ community. In this
book, we are primarily considering lesbian and gay persons in
terms of their same-sex sexuality. Same-sex sexuality is also an
aspect of bisexuality and, perhaps, an aspect of queer identity.[1]
Yet other identity labels within the full LGBTQ+ spectrum may

not involve any component of same-sex sexuality. For example, identity labels such as transgender, questioning, asexual, and intersex, while often included in the LGBTQ+ community, do not necessarily include a same-sex sexual aspect to them. Some of these are more fully represented by expanding the + in the LGBTQ+ acronym to LGBTQQIA, which refers to lesbian, gay, bisexual, transgender, queer (related to pushing back against norms associated with heterosexuality), questioning (of one's sexual identity), intersex (being born with a chromosomal, gonadal, or genetic condition that doesn't allow the person to be identified clearly as male or female at birth), and allied (or holding values that reflect an allegiance to the concerns of LGBTQ persons and their interests). Though these are often grouped together, each term names a set of remarkably different experiences. In addition, some resources will also include other identity labels, using terms such as *pansexual* (attraction to others regardless of sex or gender identity), *pangender* (or more than one gender), *gender fluid* (or gender identity that varies over time), and *gender queer* (the rejection of normative or traditional gender identities). To give just one example, people with an intersex condition will likely have a very different experience from that of a celibate gay Christian, and the celibate gay Christian's journey will likely be different again from the journey of someone who experiences gender dysphoria (distress associated with an incongruence between one's gender identity and biological sex).

Given the diversity we find within the LGBTQ+ community, is it even possible to speak of this group having a distinct culture of its own?[2] And if so, what makes LGBTQ+ culture a *culture*? For example, the African American community shares a unique cultural history in the United States, one that unites them in a shared experience. But some dimensions of LGBTQ+ history are rather dissimilar. We could compare the experience of those with varying degrees of same-sex sexuality to the experience of gender dysphoria, or cross-gender identification, or intersex conditions or asexuality, for example, and hear quite different stories.

In at least one respect, however, the LGBTQ+ community *is* a distinct culture. Insofar as it distinguishes itself from those who are heterosexual and cisgender (referring to a person whose gender identity is congruent with his or her biological sex), LGBTQ+ culture is a culture of *not being that* or not being the normative experience or majority experience of sexual orientation or gender identity. The LGBTQ+ community *as a culture* originated among those who experienced a nondominant pattern of sexual attraction, one conceptualized as a sexual orientation. In other words, the cultural narratives and values developed by those who were homosexual or bisexual *rather than* heterosexual. This communal identity was eventually expanded to note additional distinctions between male and female experiences (gay and lesbian), and expanded still further into queer identity, theory, and politics. The LGBTQ+ community then expanded to include those who are transgender (an umbrella term for many ways in which a person's gender identity does not align with their biological sex) or otherwise gender diverse, a realm that has subsequently grown to include the experiences of those whose gender is nonbinary (for example, those who identify as gender queer, gender fluid, gender creative, and gender expansive). Today this broad umbrella of identities also includes discussions of pansexuality and asexuality.

Insofar as all of these groups experienced a similar sense of exclusion from the dominant cultural narratives of sexual and gender identity, their common experience lends to the construction of a collective identity. Yet once again, we should not ignore the diversity within their experiences. This means that such an identity will invariably have its limits in determining LGBTQ+ culture. As we note elsewhere,[3] we can appreciate the desire to speak of a culture and to identify shared commonalities, but we also recognize that there may be some challenges associated with creating a culture that is most strongly defined by its contrast with existing norms of sexuality and gender.

The coalescence of LGBTQ+ persons into a culture was catalyzed by several meaningful historical events, such as the Stonewall Riots of 1969 and early organizations such as the Mattachine Society, which hoped to end criminalization of homosexual behavior. The culture-making solidarity fostered by these events and organizations expanded under the scourge of communal tragedies such as the AIDS crisis and the arrest of an estimated one hundred thousand men during the Holocaust.[4] Even today the criminalization of homosexuality still exists in some countries (including Iraq, Iran, and Saudi Arabia) and provides a culture-defining cue for LGBTQ+ individuals.

In addition, questions arise within the LGBTQ+ community around other identity markers of race and socioeconomic status. Although a full critique is beyond the scope of this project, it has been observed that the LGBTQ+ community has been shaped considerably by white gay identity and its associations with the middle class.[5] Fukuyama and Ferguson offer the following to support this view:

> Gay identity and the gay liberation movement have been associated with the White middle class. . . . [Thus] people of color may resist joining the gay liberation movement because it is perceived to be joining with the White oppressor and denying one's family ties. In some ways, a gay identity may be a function of acculturation into American society.[6]

One significant milestone in the emergence of an LGBTQ+ culture was the removal of homosexuality from the *Diagnostic and Statistical Manual of Mental Disorders (DSM)* in 1973. This early victory for gay advocates paved the way for the more robust sense of LGBTQ+ identity that would follow. While DSM changes don't create cultures, this shift in classification was an important first step, followed by moves to depathologize and later decriminalize same-sex sexual behavior. These shifts allowed for the development of a positive identity and the emergence of a community, factors that help create a possibility for a new cultural group to emerge, one that a person could positively ascribe to.

All of this is important to understand as we reflect on the experiences of celibate gay Christians. We must ask ourselves how they fit into the LGBTQ+ community. In light of the role that sexual expression has historically played in determining collective gay identity, there is a sense in which choosing celibacy out of obedience to a traditional Christian sexual ethic places celibate gay Christians in considerable contrast to what we might refer to as the "mainstream" LGBTQ+ community (where sexual expression and behavior are assumed or encouraged). In another sense, however, celibate gay Christians are still in violation of normative heterosexual identity. The relationship between LGBTQ+ culture and celibate gay Christians is a tenuous one. We have already shared some of our study participants' reflections on this tension in chapter 1.

In addition, we should be aware that celibate gay Christians are not the only group that exists in some contrast to the mainstream of the LGBTQ+ community. Those who identify as queer sometimes take issue with the political goals of gay activists, such as when these activists advocate for gay marriage. Queer theorists have historically rejected gay marriage as an egalitarian goal, one that reinforces heterosexual norms that gay people are then expected to emulate. When the United States Supreme Court ruled on *Obergefell v. Hodges* in June 2015 that gay and lesbian persons have a constitutional right to marry, this highly symbolic ruling represented the efforts of the mainstream LGBTQ+ community and their allies—indeed, it signified to a degree the successful mainstreaming of this group—but it did not mark a victory for all members of the LGBTQ+ constituency equally.

As we have discussed in greater detail elsewhere,[7] we anticipate cultural shifts in response to the Supreme Court ruling, including more media and personal exposure to gay marriage and diverse family structures. We believe that in the not-so-distant future, the terminology of "gay marriage" will be abandoned in the US and people will simply speak of "marriage," with some of those marriages between LGBTQ+ couples. Likewise, LGBTQ+ families will emerge as more visible and salient, and we will see an increasingly diverse array of family presentations marked by adoption, artificial insemination or surrogacy, and children from previous relationships.

However, there is also some evidence challenging the notion that marriage will become as common among LGBTQ+ persons as it is among straight and cisgender persons. A Gallup Poll conducted two years after the Supreme Court ruling found that 10.2 percent of LGBTQ+ Americans were married to a same-sex partner and 6.6 percent were cohabiting with a same-sex partner.[8] These numbers are lower than we might expect given rates of marrying and cohabiting among heterosexuals. Though it is still too soon after the Supreme Court ruling to know where these trends will lead, LGBTQ+ persons so far seem to be statistically more likely than their heterosexual peers to express their sexuality through singleness or noncohabiting relationships—rather than marriage.

Some of those who form the makeup of LGBTQ+ culture may reflect relationships and behaviors that are not inclined toward marriage, and this disinclination toward marriage may be the basis for what is sometimes referred to, often derogatively, as "the gay lifestyle." We would note that this disinclination toward marriage is not unique to LGBTQ+ culture. In fact, it is shared by many straight single persons as well, though their sexual decisions and preferences are not often referred to as a lifestyle in quite the same way.[9] It will be interesting to see in future years whether more LGBTQ+ persons will enter into marriage or if the marriage rates will remain modest. We do anticipate that LGBTQ+ couples and families will be increasingly visible and represent an alternative trajectory for gay people who may be considering a range of options in light of their personal and religious beliefs and values.

It has been suggested that LGBTQ+ relationships do not last as long as heterosexual ones because of higher frequencies of sex outside of the current relationship, indicating lower levels of commitment. For example, the National Lesbian Family Study[10] found that forty out of seventy-three lesbian-mother relationships dissolved by the time their child was seventeen years old. Other research, however, has shown that relationship dissolution of lesbian or gay couples is about as frequent as it is for heterosexual couples.[11] It is important to note that both studies have relatively small sample sizes, and each give their own reasoning for why the number is not higher or lower, depending on their point of view.

Whether or not gay individuals decide to marry or cohabit, the experience of being gay provides both a personal sense of identity and a corporate sense of community. We turn now to this important consideration as we take a closer look at questions about identity and the use of sexual identity labels among those who identify as celibate gay Christians.

FOUNDATIONS FOR IDENTITY AND COMMUNITY

What people share and create together can shape their thoughts, feelings, and way of experiencing the world.[12] In previous work,[13] I (Yarhouse) referred to this shaping, when it occurs among sexual minorities, as a "gay script." A script is a shorthand way of speaking of cultural expectations for behavior and relationships. Cultural expectations inform many of our behaviors, ranging from such quotidian habits as how we greet one another to major behaviors and life decisions. These behaviors and life decisions might include cultural expectations for when single people "should" marry or when married couples "should" start a family. When we discuss a gay script, then, we are discussing cultural expectations for understanding one's same-sex sexuality.

Gay Script

A gay script is a cultural expectation for making meaning out of one's experiences of same-sex attraction. It reflects contemporary meaning-making associated with same-sex sexuality. Here are a few of the assumptions and taken-for-granted realities associated with one of the predominant gay scripts[14] in the West:

- Same-sex attractions reflect categorical distinctions between types of people (lesbian, gay, bisexual, and heterosexual types of people).
- Sexual attractions signal *who you are* as a person.
- Sexual attractions reside at the core of your identity, your sense of self.
- Sexual behavior no longer resides in a category of behavior that can be evaluated as right or wrong in and of itself; rather, it is an expression of identity insofar as you express and enjoy who you really are.[15]

We are not sharing this script as something to be either embraced or rejected out of hand. Rather, we encourage thoughtful Christian engagement with the script itself. It can be helpful to understand the cultural context in which it emerged, how it has been experienced by people navigating these issues, how celibate gay Christians experience it, and so on. For those growing up in the church attracted to the same sex, a gay script may feel like a "breath of fresh air" compared to the messages they have heard about themselves from their churches.

There are, of course, multiple scripts, all with nuances that are unique to various cultures and subcultures. We might say that there is a common script derived from a person's experience in their church. This "script" would be informed by expectations that people shouldn't experience same-sex attractions, and if they do, they should work to achieve the goal of heterosexuality, viewed as synonymous with forward progress on the path of sanctification. Such a church-based script would reflect a negative view of same-sex attraction as well as specific behaviors, some of which might be drawn from an ex-gay (Side X) script that holds out expectations for orientation change or some form of healing. Of course, to be a celibate gay Christian involves following a script, a set of expectations for living with enduring same-sex sexuality while refraining from sexual behavior. Some people we interviewed expressed concern that what we refer to as a gay script could function too readily as a landing place for young people searching for identity and community. If everyone with questions or confusion about their sexuality is encouraged to embrace a gay script, then might some young people who feel confused about their sexuality prematurely self-identify as gay? This was a concern raised by Jean, a celibate gay Christian:

> [Adopting "gay" as part of my own personal identity] really took a long time, and I still leave room for believing that maybe society is too quick to call something "gay" and just go with it. "I feel this way; I'm gay; go with it." I think, tragically, that happens all too often: that high schoolers—or junior highers even, I think—maybe arrive at premature labels and don't take into account how complex it really is, how being a sexual being is a very complex thing. But I think I just try to leave room for that—that there is complexity. It's not suddenly reduced to just "gay."

Developmental psychologist Erik Erikson suggested that adolescence is a time of identity development, a time when a young person is trying to form a sense of self that is stable across relationships and settings. Adolescents who aren't experiencing same-sex attraction do not tend to identify as "gay" or to misunderstand their longings for platonic intimacy as sexual impulses. But based on Jean's comments, we recognize that this could happen, and that labels adopted prematurely may not reflect some of the complexity of identity development.

Based on our study and research among celibate gay Christians, we see some elements of the predominant gay script discussed above, but we find they do not embrace all of it. Celibate gay Christians speak of deriving some benefit from incorporating aspects of the gay script into their sense of identity, while they clearly reject other elements that reflect sexual permissiveness. Whereas those who identify as "ex-gay" must simultaneously disidentify with the gay community, celibate gay Christians intentionally draw upon elements of the gay script in their decision to identify as gay. Clearly, their decision to refrain from same-sex behavior constitutes a rejection of certain elements of the gay script. When celibate gay Christians encounter the gay script in culture, they do not approach it as an all-or-nothing proposition, something to be rejected or accepted in its entirety. Local churches often struggle with these nuances, and we suspect that the way some churches respond to celibate gay Christians reflects the binary thinking of acceptance or rejection of the gay script in general.

People navigating same-sex sexuality also have to deal with stereotypes they encounter about the LGBTQ+ community, even when these stereotypes do not match their own experience. This dynamic is unavoidable for any person who represents a numeric minority in society. Members of minority groups are sure to be stereotyped within the broader culture, and this often happens in entertainment and in the media. For example, Ben, a twenty-four-year-old Caucasian celibate man, shared this experience with regard to stereotypes about the LGBTQ+ community: "So, for me, at the time, I felt like gay meant something that I very much wasn't. It was kind of the very, very typical media stereotype. Something very flamboyant . . . the kind of character that you see on TV a lot. . . . That very much didn't resonate with who I was or I saw myself as being. Very promiscuous."

To reject stereotypes of gay identity is not the same as rejecting a gay identity. Even gay persons who do not identify as celibate may reject stereotypes of gay identity. Yet many within the LGBTQ+ community find aspects of the gay script empowering as a foundation for their identity and community. Like all gay persons, celibate gay Christians must handle questions about their own values and identities and decide where they fit within the various scripts, representations, and stereotypes of gay identity presented in the culture today.

We have seen that one of the main gay scripts in the West provides people with a sense of meaning, identity, and community. We can begin to understand how emotionally compelling the script is to people sorting out issues of sexual identity and faith. There are several additional aspects to gay scripts that relate to theories of causation and debates about orientation change. As we've mentioned, there are nuances in these discussion that are helpful to grasp as we consider the experience and perspectives of celibate gay Christians.

Theories of Causation and the Debate about Change

So far, we have been discussing how one's sense of identity can be fostered by a gay script. Yet we also want to note how a gay person's identity can be obtained (at least in part) through common assumptions about causation and change. Two prevailing assumptions have emerged in this discourse, assumptions that are typically taken for granted as unchanging realities. One of these is an assumption about the causation of same-sex attraction, and the other is an assumption about whether sexual orientation can or cannot change. These assumptions may include the belief that a person is born gay, lesbian, or bisexual—it is just a matter of discovering this about yourself. They may also include the belief that a person's attractions are a defining element of identity in part because they are enduring or immutable. What does the latest research tell us about these assumptions?

In recent research on the experiences of sexual minorities on Christian college campuses,[16] we saw that most students managing their sexual identity and faith held more biologically based beliefs about the causation and nature of same-sex attraction and did not tend to think of it as something that could change. As researchers, we are not particularly critical of these views because it is unclear from current research what causes strong, enduring same-sex sexuality. Regarding the possibility of orientation change, sexual orientation may be more mutable or fluid than frequently asserted.[17] In Lisa Diamond's research, these shifts were nonvoluntary and limited to the experiences of sexual minority females, but in general we can say that sexual orientation is probably not something that is easily changeable or likely to change categorically. In our research, we heard from many celibate gay Christians who have sought orientation change through various means (e.g., reorientation therapy, healing ministry, and so on) and have found that such approaches did not produce the outcome they were touted to produce.

What we refer to as a gay script can inform not only a person's own decision making about sexual identity and sexual behavior but also their critical assessments of other people's identities or behaviors. These assessments may include the following:

- If a person experiences same-sex attraction but does not identify as gay, lesbian, or bisexual, the belief that they are in denial or not yet ready to be honest with themselves about who they really are as a person.

- If a person experiences same-sex attraction but chooses to abstain from sexual expression, the belief that they are in denial or not yet ready to be honest with themselves about who they really are as a person.[18]

We highlight these two points because they illustrate where celibate gay Christians can have a complex relationship to the mainstream LGBTQ+ community. As noted above, many celibate gay Christians use the term *gay* to describe themselves or their same-sex sexuality, and to the extent that they do, they share that common trait with the broader LGBTQ+ community. Yet on the question of sexual expression, celibate gay Christians are by definition saying no (though imperfectly) to the taken-for-granted sexual reality of the mainstream. They do so out of a desire to say yes to something else, something tied to transcendent meaning—but the most familiar positive narratives of the gay script do not include a positive narrative like this one. In this regard, they stand apart from the mainstream LGBTQ+ identity script.

For example, Aiden, a twenty-eight-year-old Caucasian male pursuing celibacy, conveyed his experience with the expectation that he would enter into a same-sex relationship:

As much as there is to say about helping a person navigate their spirituality, when it comes down to, *Why aren't you being true to your sexuality by being in a same-sex relationship?* you are always viewed as the lesser, a person who's just not being true to himself, or is still being boxed in by conservative theology, or has been brainwashed. . . . It's really an isolating thing, to have those views that are not the case.

One interviewee, Jean, shared honestly about the difficulty of the decisions she and others face when it comes to dealing with faith and sexuality:

People in my life really have settled there [in an affirming sexual ethic]. And, yeah, honestly it makes my life . . . it's hard. I feel like, *Oh wow, it could just be so easy. Just get into one of those churches. Be embraced. Marry your partner.* You know, it's so easy and I don't even have to compromise my label as a Christian—the way I identify with my faith. I just think right now, my conscience wouldn't—I just don't think the Holy Spirit would allow that. I could do that; I just don't think I'd feel peace about it.

As we have seen, the predominant gay script has a multifaceted impact on sexual identity development. The gay script is important in part because it stands in such stark contrast to what many gay people hear from their religious faith communities growing up, and the gay script provides an alternative narrative that they may choose to adopt in part or in whole as they come to a clearer sense of self-understanding.

Those who choose not to embrace key elements of that script find themselves caught in a no-man's land between the script offered by the church and the mainstream gay script, isolated from both communities. To better understand the appeal of the LGBTQ+ community and the tension experienced by gay celibate Christians, let's take a closer look at how the LGBTQ+ community provides not only a sense of identity (vis-à-vis the gay script) but also a sense of community.

LGBTQ+ as Family

The LGBTQ+ community can be—and is often experienced or promoted as—a kind of family to people navigating same-sex sexuality. The familial welcome of this community is often contrasted with the rejection or alienation some LGBTQ+ people have experienced from their biological family. Rejection and alienation are felt most strongly when LGBTQ+ persons disclose their sexuality to their parents, which often occurs in adolescence.

Christian parents tend to experience a range of affects after such disclosures, often both positive and negative—affection for their loved one but also confusion, shock, and grief—and this ambivalence can be difficult for parents to cope with.[19] We have found that although the overall quality of parent-child relationships, and the emotional closeness in those relationships, sometimes deteriorates after disclosure, it also tends to improve over time.[20] Unfortunately, some young people do not report improvement in their relationships with their families, and for those who report high conflict, elements of that conflict can continue to the point where young persons may distance themselves from family members they do not experience as supportive. Young people who do not see improvement in their relationship with their parents often find emotional support and acceptance from the broader LGBTQ+ community, and in that sense, the LGBTQ+ community can function as surrogate family. Even when relationships with biological or legal family remain strong after coming out, the LGBTQ+ community can offer the familial comfort of being among people who share in some capacity a similar experience of the world.

Of course, not all LGBTQ+ people are alike, and we do not mean to imply that the LGBTQ+ community is a single-minded, univocal entity. Though LGBTQ+ people often find within this community the support and security of like-minded others, this does not mean that every sexual or gender minority is committed to uncritically embracing every other sexual and gender minority. There is diversity here, as there is in every other segment of the population. Yet whereas heterosexual persons can approach almost any social group with the confidence that their sexual orientation will not be grounds for exclusion from that group, same-sex-oriented persons lack that confidence. Finding community among other

LGBTQ+ persons is especially alluring, then, because it guarantees that sexual orientation will not be the sole cause of conflict that it may have been in other relationships.

Many celibate gay Christians are deeply sympathetic to the communal impulse that has brought the LGBTQ+ community together and urge their churches to recognize the admirable aspects of this community. For example, one celibate gay Christian, Aiden, spoke of the need to build bridges to the mainstream LGBTQ+ community:

> Yeah, it's really important for the church to be more involved with the LGBT community. I mean, we have a spirit day that's coming up here, next week, and it baffles me how the church, some of the people in the church fight against it—the pure goal is to show support to LGBT kids, and that we don't want them to take their own lives. Actually watching people backlash against that is really disheartening.

Aiden also acknowledged, however, that the pursuit of common ground between straight Christians and sexual minorities is made more difficult by historic tensions that have persisted into the present day:

> There's already miles of bad blood between the church and the LGBT community because of what's happened in the past. When you look back, when the LGBT community went through the AIDS crisis, and the effect the conservative Christian televangelist community had in consulting with the Reagan administration to not advocate for the needs of people who are dying every day from AIDS, was just huge. We are still living with the effects of that.

Our cultural history sets a background of mistrust and a lack of communication between different groups and stakeholders that persists to this day. As we approach this subject, we should promote empathetic understanding among various groups and engage them in dialogue, bearing in mind that the cultural gap may not be easy to bridge and will require wisdom and patience.

CONCLUSION

The prospect of bridging these two communities—the sexually "conservative" Christian community and the mainstream LGBTQ+ community—is beyond the scope of this book. For many youth sorting out sexual-or gender-identity questions, the differences between the local church and the broader LGBTQ+ community appear stark and irreconcilable. The church is likely to be perceived as a place of silence or condemnation—even for those who have same-sex attractions yet remain celibate. The LGBTQ+ community, on the other hand, is often described as "the family" and provides a person a sense of both identity and community—two of the most important commodities to any young person today. Despite the many ways in which celibate gay Christians find themselves at odds with the predominant values of the broader LGBTQ+ community, they may yet receive a warmer welcome from the LGBTQ+ community than they do from their Christian communities.

FOR DISCUSSION

1. How would you describe what we refer to as a gay script? What might make the gay script emotionally compelling to someone navigating same-sex sexuality?
2. How are theories of causation related to the gay script?
3. How would you connect the debate about whether people can change their sexual orientation to the gay script? Why does the debate about change of orientation matter to celibate gay Christians?

4. How would you describe a church script or ex-gay script? How about a celibate gay Christian script? What are the cultural expectations embedded in each script?
5. How would you describe how celibate gay Christians are a part of the LGBTQ+ community and ways in which they do not always seem to reflect the assumptions of the LGBTQ+ community?

CHAPTER 3

EXPERIENCES *of* CELIBATE GAY CHRISTIANS

In the first chapter we introduced the terminology of Sides A, B, C, and X as a shorthand for conveying contrasting theological positions. We noted that these terms originated with the Bridges Across the Divide Project[1] and have been used by the Gay Christian Network (which changed leadership in 2017 and transitioned to Q Christian Fellowship) and others to clarify different beliefs about homosexuality among Christians in the gay community. These organizations intentionally chose to move away from *pro-gay* and *anti-gay* terminology, terms that demonstrate a preference based on language (similar to how *pro-choice* or *pro-life* language shapes perceptions in the abortion debate). In search of neutral terminology, they created the terms *Side A* (the belief that some same-sex sexual relationships can be morally permissible) and *Side B* (the belief that same-sex sexual relationships are morally impermissible). Other "sides" were subsequently added as well: *Side C* refers to those who are either undecided or in tension around sexual ethics. *Side X* refers to those who believe a Christian should disidentify with a gay identity and pursue heterosexuality.

Using these categories, celibate gay Christians are thought of as Side B gay Christians. They believe that same-sex genital relationships are morally impermissible. Some Side B Christians may abstain from *any* romantic relationships, while others engage in heterosexual relationships and even marry, which is sometimes referred to as mixed-orientation marriage. However, it is important to note that Side B Christians are not trying to become straight. They are simply committed to living according to a traditional Christian sexual ethic in which sexual behavior is reserved for marriage between a man and a woman, whether this ethic means that they will be called to celibacy or to a mixed-orientation marriage with an opposite-sex partner.

In a recent talk[2] on sexual identity and Christianity, a popular Christian speaker who has been outspoken about her own repentance from homosexuality and a lesbian identity through the power of the gospel, presented a strong critique of gay Christianity and the Side B perspective. She brought a strong charge against Wesley Hill and others from the Spiritual Friendship[3] movement, Side B believers who are attempting to live chaste lives as celibate gay Christians. Here is an excerpt of the critique:

> I shudder to think about how much more rigorous, painful, dangerous, and difficult my conversion would have been had it taken place in 2016. . . . Why? Well, if my conversion to Christ had played out in 2016 and not in 1999 . . . likely I might have been told that I was really a gay Christian. . . .
>
> I likely would have been told I was just a gay Christian and there are two tracks of life for a gay Christian like me. I can have "Side A" with Matthew Vines, Justin Lee, and the Gay Christian Network, embracing a revisionist biblical understanding that Scripture is neither inerrant, inspired, nor trustworthy and that affirms the goodness of gay sexual practices and relationships. Or, hey, I could go "Side B" with Wesley Hill and the Spiritual Friendship gang, where I would learn that my sexual desires for women were actually

sanctifiable and redeemable, making me a better friend to
one and all. But for the sake of Christian tradition, I should
not act on them. . . .

I think that sexual strugglers need gay Christianity and
all of its attending liberal sellouts, including the "Side B"
version, like fish need bicycles. . . .

While some people see a world of difference between
acting on unholy desires and simply cherishing them in your
heart, our Lord would say otherwise. . . .

The differences that separate the factions of gay Christianity, the differences between Matthew Vines and Wes Hill,
take place on a razor's edge.

The speaker's primary criticism seems to be that Side B seeks
to redeem or positively portray the sexual desires an individual
feels for a person of the same sex. Her concern is that by seeking
to sanctify same-sex sexual desires through celibacy and friendship
and by adopting the adjective *gay* as a descriptor of a person's
identity, the Side B perspective risks leading people astray from
biblical truth, from the value of repentance, and from the power
of the gospel itself. She further suggests that what celibate gay
Christians are doing is dangerous, or at the very least confusing
and unnecessary. Although we are unable to offer a full critique of
this speaker's position, we want to note that it is not uncommon
for someone to use God's work in their own life as a standard by
which they measure what should be expected from others (and
what pastors should allow in their pastoral care). Exhortation
rooted in personal experience can be well intentioned, but it can
have pitfalls as well. Developing a universal standard based on a
personal journey can lead to condemnation of those who try and
fail to achieve the same outcome. At its worst, such an approach
builds walls around the gospel by denying the diversity of ways in
which God works in different people's lives.

In saying this, we are not defending the theology associated with a Side A perspective. We are simply saying that many gay Christians who pursue a life of chastity (those designated as Side B in her talk) believe in the power of the gospel and live a life of repentance. To suggest to them that their efforts have been insufficient may not be the appropriate response. Chiding pastors who make room for gay Christians pursuing celibacy seems counterproductive.

In a book of his collected letters, Henri Nouwen wrote to a woman who was critical of Nouwen for not "taking the correct approach to healing himself."[4] Here is an excerpt from Nouwen's response:

> Your statement that my vision of God is askew, that the emotional imagery of my heart is also askew and I simply need to become available for healing, feels really quite distant and makes me feel somewhat condemned. It simply sounded like: "You know there must be other healing available for you; why don't you get your act together and accept the healing that is there for you." If you had any idea of what I have been struggling with over the past eight months and how I have been trying to really enter into the furnace of God's love and give up everything else in order to really let God heal me, you probably never would have written these words.[5]

Nouwen did not describe himself as a "gay Christian" or a "celibate gay Christian," yet we are struck by the fact that Nouwen was criticized by fellow Christians for his decision to live a celibate Christian life while struggling with unremitting same-sex desire. Those who make such attacks want to hear a testimony of healing—that is, a testimony of homosexual desire being replaced by heterosexual desire—and they place the responsibility for the lack of healing on the gay individual. Notice Nouwen's charity toward the woman who made the charge. His response attempts to foster in her some cognitive complexity about the long-term nature of the struggle he faced:

> I know that you don't want to hurt me and that you do care for me. So I hope that you also can be patient and trust that God will do his work when His time comes. It quite easily might take another ten or twenty years until the deepest wounds in me are healed. *It might even be that God wants to teach me how to live with them as a way to participate in the suffering of Jesus.* I really don't know, but, healing or no healing, I trust that God is greater than my heart and that He desires to show me His love.[6]

In sharing this brief mention of some of the criticism of the gay celibate or Side B movement, our purpose is not to wade into all of the theological arguments or propose a simple answer to a complex issue. We want to suggest that compassion and understanding are needed, that perhaps the church is at its best when it recognizes the different ways in which God responds to the cries of his people. Our hope is that together we can agree that God is sovereign and is working out his purposes in the lives of those who, often out of a place of great anguish, are bringing their requests to him.

WHAT DOES IT MEAN TO BE A CELIBATE GAY CHRISTIAN?

What does it mean to be a celibate gay Christian? In what follows we will unpack each of these phrases and offer you a snapshot of some of the findings of our study and who participated.

They Are Celibate

Our study is the largest study to date of the newly emerging group calling themselves "celibate gay Christians." As they define themselves—a definition we are adopting for the purpose of this study—celibate gay Christians are people who experience same-sex attraction to such a degree that they would think of themselves as oriented toward the same sex, and they align themselves with the Christian faith in such a way that they have concluded that same-sex sexual relationships are morally impermissible; as a result, they have committed themselves to refraining from same-sex genital intimacy.

When we set out to conduct our study, part of a larger line of research on various dimensions of the celibate gay Christian experience, we envisioned participants of our study as gay Christians who were refraining from all sexual intimacy. We found when we launched the study that the largest segment of our sample, 166 of 300 (or 55 percent of the sample), identified as celibate from same-sex relationships. That is, they refrain from same-sex genital sexual intimacy. However, they indicated that they were *open to a relationship with the opposite sex*, as contrasted with those who do not see such a relationship as an option. Another 66 participants indicated that they refrained from all sexual intimacy and were not open to a heterosexual relationship (most of these, 57, identified as male, while 9 identified as female).

Some of our participants reported that they are in a mixed-orientation marriage. A mixed-orientation marriage is one in which one partner is same-sex attracted (or gay) and their spouse is attracted to the opposite sex (or heterosexual). In fact, another 66 participants indicated that they were gay in a marriage with a spouse who is straight (most of these, 56, identified as male, while 9 identified as female and 1 as transgender). What they appear to be saying is that they define celibacy as refraining from sexual intimacy with someone of the same sex. Because the majority of Side B gay Christians—including many of those who are most visible in public dialogue—are unmarried and celibate, gay Christians in mixed-orientation marriages may sometimes align themselves with the "celibate gay Christian" label for the sake of ease, even though they are not celibate in the traditional sense of the word (refraining from all sexual activity). The average number of years respondents were celibate was twenty-one years (SD = 16)[7] for those who indicated they are celibate from all sexual relationships. For those who indicated they are celibate from same-sex relationships only, the average time celibate was twenty years (SD = 13).

They Are Gay

When we refer to celibate gay Christians, we use the word *gay* to convey, at minimum, a person's sexual orientation, even though *gay* can mean more than that, as we will discuss in subsequent chapters. When asked about their sexual orientation, the vast majority (244, or 81 percent) identified as having a homosexual orientation, suggesting an essentially exclusive attraction to the same sex. Fifty-nine (19.6 percent) identified as bisexual, and one person identified as "celibate" but did not specify sexual orientation.

We asked participants to share with us the strength of their attraction to both the same sex and the opposite sex. They rated their attractions on two 10-point scales, representing the percentage of time they experience attraction to the opposite and same sex. The anchors were a score of 0 percent (no attraction) to 100 percent (all the time). We then divided up the scores to reflect low (0–30 percent), medium (40–60 percent), and high (70–100 percent) attraction. We found that 84 percent of our sample scored high in same-sex attraction, while 10 percent fell in the medium and 5.7 percent in the low same-sex attraction category. There were no differences in attraction levels between the group that was celibate from all sexual relationships and those who were celibate only from same-sex sexual relationships. The only significant difference was between these two groups and those who were in a mixed-orientation marriage or relationship. Of these participants, 69.7 percent scored in the high same-sex attraction category, while 22.7 percent were in the medium and 7.6 percent in the low same-sex attraction category. With respect to opposite-sex attraction, only 4.7 percent of our sample scored in the high range in attraction to the opposite sex, whereas 8.7 percent scored in the medium and 86.7 percent fell in the low opposite-sex attraction range. Again, the main difference we saw among our three groups was between those in mixed-orientation marriages and the other two groups. Of those in mixed-orientation marriages, 10.6 percent reported being high in attraction to the opposite sex, 24.2 percent were medium, and 65.2 percent were low in attraction to the opposite sex.

In our previous research on sexual minorities at Christian colleges and universities, we reported comparable findings: on a 10-point scale of same-sex and opposite-sex attractions, the mean score for attraction to the same sex was 8.0 (SD = 2.3) and for attraction to the opposite sex was 4.9 (SD = 3.3). Nearly 70 percent (69.4 percent) experienced more same-sex attraction than opposite-sex attraction. Few held attractions to the same and opposite sex equally (8.1 percent), and 22.5 percent were more attracted to the opposite sex than to the same sex. Perhaps the greatest difference between these two studies was the finding that as people left college and grew older, they developed more clarity around the question of whether they would choose to be celibate, pursue a mixed-orientation marriage, or remain open to both possibilities.

To investigate the importance of specific labels for celibate gay Christians, we asked them to compare how strongly they identified with the labels "Christian," "gay," "gay Christian," and "celibate gay Christian." They told us that what was most important to them was to identify as a Christian—while they found some or all of the other labels useful from time to time, they ranked "Christian" as the label they identified with the highest percentage of the time. It did not matter whether they were celibate from all relationships, celibate from same-sex relationships (but open to a relationship with the opposite sex), or in a mixed-orientation relationship or marriage; all three groups valued their Christian identity most highly.

Our sample also surprised us by not valuing the labels *gay, gay Christian*, and *celibate gay Christian* as highly as we thought they would. Given the nature of many discussions about sexuality, we thought this group would place a higher emphasis on the importance of these words. We found, however, that these identity labels were of medium or high importance only to about 40 percent of those we surveyed. Thus, while a sizable minority did find the words necessary and salient, appearing regularly in their vocabulary, about 60 percent considered them to be of low importance.

They Are Christian

Our sample of celibate gay Christians is mostly Protestant. Of our 300-person sample, 243, or 81 percent, identified as Protestant, a large umbrella that includes a wide range of denominations including Lutheran, Anglican, Reformed, Baptist, and nondenominational. Another 45 participants (15 percent) identified as Catholic, while 6 identified as Orthodox and another 6 came from other Christian traditions.

On two scales that asked about religiosity and spirituality (ranging from 1, "Not religious or spiritual," to 10, "Very religious or spiritual"), our sample identified as both highly religious and highly spiritual. In terms of religiosity, 89 percent of our sample reported themselves as between 7 and 10 on the 10-point scale. The response for spirituality was even higher, with 93 percent of our sample reporting themselves as between 7 and 10 on the 10-point scale.

We asked participants to complete the Duke University Religiosity Index, or the DUREL.[8] This included questions on church attendance, personal religious practices (such as prayer), and attitudinal statements (such as "I try hard to carry my religion over into all other dealings in life").

When we asked participants about church attendance, 91 percent of our sample indicated going to church once a week or more, which is considered to be high. We see a little more diversity of practice when it comes to prayer, meditation, and Bible study. Regarding prayer, most (67 percent) identified high engagement in prayer, meaning they prayed daily or more frequently than that. About a quarter (26 percent) were moderate, praying at least once weekly. There was more of a split with meditation and Bible study. With meditation, 26 percent fell in the high range (daily or more), 34 percent in the medium (weekly), and 40 percent in the low (never or rarely). Similarly, with Bible study, we found that 34 percent studied the Bible daily or more, 43 percent weekly, and 23 percent never or rarely.

In the attitudinal statements, 82 percent felt that they experience the presence of the divine, responding that this either "tends to be true" or is "definitely true of me." Participants also responded to the statement, "My religious beliefs are what really lie behind my whole approach to life." This was true for 95 percent of our sample (from "tends to be true" to "definitely true for me"). In response to the statement, "I try hard to carry my religion over into all other dealings in life," 81 percent found this to be true for them (from "tends to be true" to "definitely true for me").

What we can conclude from these measures is that our sample of celibate gay Christians is highly religious. They are not Christians only in name or by upbringing or by some other cultural factor. Rather, they are highly intrinsically religious, meaning that their faith deeply impacts all aspects of their lives, including decisions they make about sexuality and sexual behavior. They are predominantly regular churchgoers who are engaged in daily or weekly devotional practices.

Additional Demographics

The majority of our sample are gay males (n = 245, or 82 percent), while 52 participants identified as female, and 3 as transgender.

In terms of age, the average age was thirty-four (SD = 13), where 210, or 70 percent, of the participants were under age forty, and 156, or 52 percent, of the overall sample were under age thirty. Some readers may wonder how our participants' views on celibacy will shift as they enter their forties or fifties. Perhaps they are too young to really know what they are committing themselves to. We acknowledge that as a possibility and admit we are limited by the design of the study: we are not tracking celibate gay Christians over several years to see whether and how their experience of celibacy changes over time. On the other hand, if we had an older sample—say, one with a mean age of fifty or sixty—we would also be facing the challenge of representing what celibacy has meant to Christians in previous generations, when there was a greater emphasis on reparative therapy and healing ministries. As it stands, we suspect that our younger demographic reflects some of the cultural shifts in Christian circles that have brought about the rise of the celibate gay Christian movement. These cultural shifts have become more visible in recent years, influenced (as we have argued in chapter 1) by the closing of Exodus International, the flagship ex-gay umbrella ministry, as well as by a rise in ex-ex-gay testimonies (of persons who at one time identified as ex-gay but then recanted), a diminished ex-gay narrative, and an increase in questions about how to live with an enduring reality of same-sex sexuality. Studying a relatively young sample, as we have done, may give us a deepened understanding of how these recent developments have shaped the perspectives of sexual minorities.

In terms of race and ethnicity, the majority of our sample (256, or 85.3 percent) identified as European American. Twenty-two participants (7.3 percent) identified as Asian/Pacific Islander, while 10 (3.3 percent) identified as multiracial, 8 (2.6 percent) as African-American, and 4 (<1 percent) as Hispanic/Latino.

WHAT DO CELIBATE GAY CHRISTIANS BELIEVE?

We asked celibate gay Christians about their attitudes and beliefs on a range of topics. We gave each individual a statement or question about something like the causes of same-sex attraction, and then they were asked to select a response from a six-point Likert scale that ranged from "strongly disagree" to "strongly agree." Following are several of the topics we asked them about.

Are Same-Sex Attractions and Behavior Sin?

One controversy in the debates about sexuality and sexual identity in the church is the question of whether same-sex attraction itself is sin. You may recall that many of the pastors we interviewed had imprecise responses, often conflating attraction and behavior. We asked the celibate gay Christians in our study to respond to the following statement: "Being attracted sexually to members of the same gender is morally acceptable." This statement elicited the greatest diversity of responses. About two-thirds of the entire sample (65 percent) agreed with this (strongly, moderately, or slightly), whereas 35 percent of the entire sample disagreed with this (strongly, moderately, or slightly). Looking more closely at the three groups we have outlined—those who are celibate from all relationships; those who are celibate from same-sex relationships; and those who are in mixed-orientation marriages—we notice some differences. Those who are celibate from all relationships were much more likely to agree (83 percent) that being attracted sexually to members of the same gender is morally acceptable, compared to those who were celibate from same-sex relationships but open to opposite-sex relationships (63 percent) or those who were in mixed-orientation marriages (55 percent). While there tends to be agreement among those in mixed-orientation marriages, the fact that a smaller percentage find same-sex attraction to be morally acceptable may have contributed to some extent to same-sex-attracted Christians making the decision to enter into a mixed-orientation relationship.

We also provided a statement about same-sex behavior: "Sexual behavior between members of the same gender is morally acceptable." Here we saw a far greater consensus: 90 percent of our sample disagreed with this statement, and we saw great consistency across all categories of participants. Likewise, we provided a statement specifically addressing monogamous same-sex relationships, as such relationships are often a consideration for a Christian who experiences same-sex attraction and is considering celibacy. The statement was: "Monogamous sexual relationships between members of the same gender can be blessed, or receive God's grace and love." Again, most of our participants (86 percent) disagreed with this statement, with little variation across groups. Anywhere from 12 percent to 20 percent across our three groups agreed with the statement.

What Causes Same-Sex Attraction?

Some of the cultural and scientific debate on the topic of same-sex attraction has revolved around causation and change. What causes same-sex sexuality, and can sexual attractions or orientation change? To address this issue we provided three different but related statements about causation. The first had to do with choice: "Persons can choose who they are sexually attracted to." A full 91 percent of our sample disagreed with this statement. The only real variation was between those who were in a mixed-orientation marriage (83 percent disagreed) and those who were celibate from all relationships (97 percent), with those who were celibate but open to a mixed-orientation relationship falling in between (91 percent). Still, across all three categories, most disagreed with the idea that a person can choose who they are sexually attracted to.

Another statement we provided was, "Persons who experience same-sex attraction could have been born with this predisposition." This statement refers to the biological hypothesis that something like prenatal hormonal exposure or a genetic predisposition could provide a "push" toward same-sex attraction for some people.[9] Most of our sample (88 percent) agreed with this statement, with only slight variations between 87 percent and 91 percent across our three groups.

The third and final statement regarding causation had to do with the environment, which is often set in contrast to biology in the "nature versus nurture" debate. "Experience/environment plays a greater role in the development of same-sex attraction than does biology." In response to this statement, 58 percent agreed, while 42 percent disagreed. Although fewer celibate gay Christians agreed than did those in the other two categories, there were no statistically significant differences here. A range of opinions was represented across all three groupings.

Can People Change Their Attractions to the Same Sex?

Regarding the debate about orientation change, we provided the following statement: "Persons who experience same-sex attraction can change this aspect of their attractions to the opposite sex." Most of our sample (82 percent) disagreed with this statement. However, this was the other item that had a statistically significant difference across our three groupings. Celibate gay Christians were far more likely to disagree with the statement—a full 96 percent disagreeing with it—whereas only 69 percent of people in mixed-orientation marriages disagreed. Falling in between, 82 percent of those who are celibate from same-sex relationships but open to opposite-sex relationships disagreed. Though most of our sample disagrees with the idea that a person can change their attractions to the same sex, there were some nuances here; those in a mixed-orientation marriage were most likely (though still unlikely) to express agreement.

We also asked whether people can live a celibate life. Is celibacy even possible? The statement we provided was, "Persons can live a sexually celibate life while they have same-sex attraction." We see much more consensus here, as 99 percent of our sample indicated agreement with this statement. Interestingly, only three people disagreed with the statement: one from each of the three groups.

Despite the fact that our sample overwhelmingly believes that people can live a sexually celibate life, this question is likely to be one of the two most highly scrutinized questions in this study: "Is it possible to live a celibate life?" The other is this: "Is it healthy to live a celibate life?" We believe these questions will be closely examined because relatively little research is available to help us answer them. Most research on celibacy has explored priestly celibacy, specifically the experience of Roman Catholic priests who take a vow of celibacy and who presumably have a sense of call and some institutional support to live out that call, combined with a religious sense of transcendent meaning and purpose. Although we are unable to provide an in-depth analysis of the findings on Roman Catholic priests and celibacy, we want to reflect on a few of the studies that have been conducted. Some of this research took place following the sex abuse scandal that shook the Roman Catholic Church, as in the wake of this scandal many people expressed concern about whether being celibate was healthy. Some wondered if the doctrine that supported celibacy was detrimental or erroneous because it set a standard that people could not reasonably achieve, a standard that was unhealthy even to pursue.

Perhaps the most sobering reflection on the state of celibacy in the Roman Catholic priesthood has come from Richard Sipe,[10] himself a former priest. Drawing upon ethnographic research from more than twenty-five years of experience, Sipe made the following estimates: "About 20 percent of priests vowed to celibacy . . . are at any one time involved either in a more or less stable sexual relationship with a woman or, alternatively, with sequential women in an identifiable pattern of behavior. An additional 8 to 10 percent of priests are at a stage of heterosexual exploration that often involves incidental sexual contacts."[11] These "incidental sexual contacts" might be "dating" or "pre-dating" behaviors that may or may not evolve into sexual behaviors.[12] Sipe later wrote, "Generally, 18 to 22 percent of clergy . . . are either involved in homosexual relationships, have a conflict about periodic sexual activity, feel compelled toward homosexual involvements, identify themselves as homosexual, or at least have serious questions about their sexual orientation or differentiation."[13] Granted, Sipe cast a wide-ranging net that includes many possible experiences, ranging from actively engaging in same-sex relationships to self-identifying as homosexual to having questions about sexual orientation.

Regarding masturbation, Sipe views self-stimulation as "the most common and frequently used sexual behavior of celibates."[14] He estimates that "20 percent of priests are involved in masturbatory patterns that are manifestations of sexual immaturity," such as overusing self-stimulation as "an exclusive tension-reducing maneuver" and exhibiting a "preference of sexual fantasy over sexual reality."[15] He also notes that this 20 percent does not include other celibate priests involved in other (partnered) sexual behaviors that may involve masturbation. Many priests apparently do not see self-stimulation as a sin, although some do, and many do not see it as a sign of immaturity, although, again, some do. Other researchers who have studied celibate priests have offered comparable estimates regarding sexual activity.[16] Based on these studies, it seems that complete abstinence from sexual activity is possible for many, but variations in what constitutes abstinence have also been recorded among those seeking to pursue a celibate life.

For people who pursue lifelong celibacy, the question remains: Is living a life of celibacy healthy? Some of the studies that have attempted to answer this question use rather imprecise measures and often rely on a Freudian psychoanalytic understanding of psychosexual development—an understanding that is no longer prominent among psychologists—to define what counts as healthy development and maturity. Other studies discuss these same concerns without relying so heavily on a specific tradition for interpreting what counts as maturity. One of the more widely cited studies on health and celibacy comes from Kennedy and Heckler,[17] who reported data from interviews with 271 priests. These authors concluded that perhaps as many as two-thirds of priests may be considered psychologically or socially underdeveloped—that is, having "not completed the tasks which are appropriate to the developmental period known as adolescence."[18] Again, some of these conclusions are framed in language that may be foreign to a large number of mental-health professionals today.

In response to these data, some have advised that Roman Catholics should revisit their institutional commitment to celibacy for priests, while others have proposed more robust ways to support and strengthen that commitment. For example, Sonny Manuel,[19] who is both a priest and a psychologist, offers his own suggestions for how to foster healthy celibacy. He suggests that healthy celibate persons must have a close relationship with God that includes reflection on one's decision to place desire for God above all other desires. In addition, communities and relationships of support that have both breadth and depth are needed, as well as the ability to ask for love and nurture from others. Manuel advocates for the development of healthy coping behaviors and ongoing spiritual discipline. We will return to these and other suggestions as we consider how to provide tangible support at an individual and institutional level for celibate gay Christians.

In summary, it is unclear how representative these findings are for Roman Catholic priests, let alone for others pursuing celibacy for a range of reasons. All that we can confidently say is that the question of how celibate gay Christians are doing emotionally needs further exploration.

HOW ARE CELIBATE GAY CHRISTIANS DOING EMOTIONALLY?

Many people are skeptical of the idea that celibacy is healthy. They assume it is a foregone conclusion that abstaining from sexual activity is detrimental to a person. However, we see this as an empirical question worth asking and attempting to answer. To that end, we have invited celibate gay Christians to tell us about their experiences and to provide information on measures of well-being, such as depression, anxiety, stress, and other possible symptoms of distress. The measures we used were the Depression, Anxiety and Stress Scale (DASS-21), the Counseling Center Assessment of Psychological Symptoms (CCAPS), the Personal Well-Being Scale, and the Ryff Emotional Well-Being Scale. We will look first at the symptoms of psychological concerns, such as depression and anxiety, before we look at personal and emotional well-being.

Depression, anxiety, and stress. We asked participants to complete the Depression, Anxiety and Stress Scale (DASS-21). The DASS-21 measures the severity of a person's depression, anxiety, and stress as either normal (the lowest rating), mild, moderate, or severe (the highest rating). Overall, we found that our sample of celibate gay Christians was healthier than might be expected, given the complexities of their social position relative to Christian and LGBTQ+ communities. About 80 percent (79.1 percent) fell in the normal range for depression, with another 12 percent in the mild range, 8 percent in the moderate range, and 1 percent in the severe range (see table 3.1). For comparison, major depressive disorder is diagnosed in about 7 percent of the general population, with higher prevalence for adults under thirty years of age.[20] While DASS does not provide a precise gauge for major depressive disorder diagnosis, the moderate and severe depression ratings in our study were in the same ballpark with higher depression levels for those who were celibate from all relationships (12.3 percent), though still rather low (see table 3.2). Even higher percentages of our participants scored in the normal range for anxiety and stress. For anxiety, 93 percent were in the normal range, while 3 percent were in mild, 4 percent in moderate, and less than 1 percent in severe. For stress, 94 percent were in the normal range, while

5 percent were in mild, less than 1 percent in moderate, and none in severe.

TABLE 3.1. DEPRESSION, ANXIETY, AND STRESS BY SEVERITY RATING

Severity Rating	Depression		Anxiety		Stress	
	n	Percent	n	Percent	n	Percent
Normal	235	79	275	93	280	94
Mild	35	12	9	3	15	5
Moderate	24	8	11	4	2	<1
Severe	3	1	2	<1	0	0

Depression appears to be the highest risk among our participants. Of the three groups we surveyed, those who identified as celibate from all sexual relationships were most at risk of depression (see table 3.2). Of these celibate gay Christians, 68 percent scored in the normal range for depression, 20 percent in the mild range, 12 percent in the moderate range, and none in the severe range, and the differences were not statistically significant.

TABLE 3.2. DEPRESSION RATINGS BY CELIBACY TYPE

Depression Severity Rating	Celibate from All		Celibate from Same Sex		Mixed-Orientation Marriage	
	n	Percent	n	Percent	n	Percent
Normal	44	67.7	136	81.4	55	84.6
Mild	13	20.0	17	10.2	5	7.7
Moderate	8	12.3	12	7.2	4	6.2
Severe	0	0	2	1.2	1	1.5

Assessment of psychological symptoms. The Counseling Center Assessment of Psychological Symptoms (CCAPS)[21] is another measure we asked participants to complete to get a sense of their psychological health. This instrument was originally developed to measure a range of mental health concerns (e.g., depression, generalized anxiety, social anxiety) that a sample of students presented with when seeking mental health services at their colleges and universities.

Our results were mixed, as might be anticipated, with some areas of potential concern and others looking better than expected. Taken together, most of our sample of celibate gay Christians scored in the normal range, which might be better than many would assume. For example, on the Distress Index, which is a combination of selected items from measures of depression, social and general anxiety, academic distress, and hostility, 92 percent were in the normal range and only 8 percent were elevated (see table 3.3). If we look at each scale individually, we see higher percentages elevated in depression (24 percent elevated), social anxiety (28 percent elevated), and eating concerns (25 percent elevated). Despite these elevations, this means that 76 percent of our overall sample were in the normal range for depression; 72 percent were in the normal range for social anxiety; and 75 percent were in the normal range for eating concerns. Please note that this measure does not allow for the symptom severity-level separation (mild, moderate, or severe) and only indicates the presence or absence of elevated scores.

TABLE 3.3. CCAPS INDEX SCORES FOR PSYCHOLOGICAL SYMPTOMS

Subscales	Normal		Elevated	
	n	Percent	n	Percent
Depression	226	76.1	71	23.9
Generalized Anxiety	271	91.2	26	8.8
Social Anxiety	215	72.4	82	27.6
Academic Distress	272	91.6	25	8.4

TABLE 3.3 *(continued)*

Subscales	Normal		Elevated	
	n	Percent	n	Percent
Eating Concerns	224	75.4	73	24.6
Hostility	282	94.9	15	5.1
Alcohol Use	276	93.2	20	6.8
Distress Index	272	91.6	25	8.4

As with our previous measures, some differences are more pronounced based on type of celibacy (see table 3.4). For example, a higher percentage of those who identified as celibate from all relationships were more elevated in depression (37 percent) and social anxiety (39 percent). Among those who identified as celibate from same-sex relationships but open to other relationships, elevations were 21 percent for depression and 26 percent for social anxiety. The likelihood for elevations was even lower for those in mixed-orientation marriages: 19 percent for depression and 20 percent for social anxiety.

It is also possible to look at psychological health in terms of what is going well for celibate gay Christians rather than what is not. Toward that end, we looked at well-being, which includes strengths that are present rather than symptoms that suggest deficits.

Personal well-being. We administered a measure of personal well-being that looked at how people report their own satisfaction in a number of areas of life, including standard of living, health, personal relationships, and feeling part of a community. One final question asked participants to rank their "life as a whole" as a way of summarizing all these facets of living taken together. An average Western population responding to this measure will indicate that they are satisfied with life between 70 percent and 80 percent of the time.[22] Satisfaction scores between 70 percent and 100 percent are coded as high, scores between 40 percent and 60 percent are medium, and scores between 0 percent and 30 percent are low.

TABLE 3.4. CCAPS INDEX SCORE PERCENTAGES BY CELIBACY TYPE

Subscales	Celibate from All		Celibate from Same Sex		Mixed-Orientation Marriage	
	Normal	Elevated	Normal	Elevated	Normal	Elevated
Depression	63.1[a,b]	36.9	79.0[a]	21.0	81.5[b]	18.5
Generalized Anxiety	90.8	9.2	92.2	7.8	89.2	10.8
Social Anxiety	61.5[b]	38.5	73.7	26.3	80.0[b]	20.0
Academic Distress	84.6[b]	15.4	92.8	7.2	95.4[b]	4.6
Eating Concerns	75.4	24.6	75.4	24.6	75.4	24.6
Hostility	95.4	4.6	95.2	4.8	93.8	6.2
Alcohol Use	90.6	9.4	94.0	6.0	93.8	6.2
Distress Index	85.6[a]	15.4	93.4[a]	6.6	93.8	6.2

Note[a,b]: Statistically significant group differences with $p \leq .05$

TABLE 3.5. PERSONAL WELL-BEING

Percentage of Time Satisfied with:	High		Medium		Low	
	n	Percent	n	Percent	n	Percent
Standard of Living	228	78.8	51	17.2	18	6.1
Health	202	68.0	71	23.9	24	8.1
Achieving in Life	162	54.5	93	31.3	42	14.1
Personal Relationships	145	48.8	93	31.3	59	19.9
Safety	239	80.5	39	13.1	19	6.4

TABLE 3.5 *(continued)*

Percentage of Time Satisfied with:	High		Medium		Low	
	n	Percent	n	Percent	n	Percent
Feeling Part of Your Community	140	47.1	93	31.3	64	21.5
Future Security	128	43.4	95	32.2	72	24.4
Personal Spirituality or Religion	228	76.8	51	17.2	18	6.1
Life as a Whole	189	63.6	79	26.6	29	9.8

When people rated their overall personal well-being (answering the question about "life as a whole"), we found that life satisfaction was high for 64 percent of the sample (see table 3.5). Another 27 percent rated their well-being in the medium range. Only 10 percent were in the low range. People in mixed-orientation marriages were mostly likely to rank their personal well-being highly. Indeed, 75 percent of participants in mixed-orientation marriages scored high on personal well-being, compared to 64 percent of those celibate from same-sex relationships but open to opposite-sex relationships and 53 percent of those celibate from all relationships. Even in the lowest-scoring group, over half of those who are celibate from all sexual relationships scored high on personal well-being; however, 29 percent of this group were in the medium range, and a sizable minority (19 percent) were in the low range.

What aspects of personal well-being did people struggle with most? We can get a sense of this by evaluating their answers to specific survey items. All three groups reported lower rates of personal well-being in the areas of personal relationships, feeling part of their community, and future security. In all three areas, fewer than half of our participants ranked themselves as highly satisfied. In addition, if we look at the median scores on personal well-being by celibacy type, we see further evidence of differences among our three groups (see table 3.6). Indeed, none of the areas fall below 70 for those in mixed-orientation marriages. In contrast, those who are celibate from all relationships and those who are celibate from same-sex relationships fall below 70 in the areas of personal relationships, feeling part of their community, and future security, and those who are celibate from all relationships also fell below 70 in the area of achieving in life.

TABLE 3.6. MEDIAN SCORES ON PERSONAL WELL-BEING BY CELIBACY TYPE

Percentage of Time Satisfied with:	Celibate from All	Celibate from Same Sex	Mixed-Orientation Marriages
	Median	Median	Median
Standard of Living	80	80	80
Health	80	80	80
Achieving in Life	60	70	75
Personal Relationships	60	60	70
Safety	80	90	90
Feeling Part of Your Community	50	60	70
Future Security	60	60	70
Personal Spirituality or Religion	80	80	90
Life as a Whole	70	70	80

Psychological well-being. Our sample of celibate gay Christians also completed a measure of psychological well-being (Ryff-54, Ryff;[23] Ryff and Keyes[24]). The Ryff-54 assesses various dimensions of psychological well-being by having participants rate their agreement with each of its fifty-four items on a six-point Likert scale, ranging from *1 = strongly disagree* to *6 = strongly agree.* As with our previous research[25] with sexual minority students at Christian colleges, only three subscales were utilized in the current study: (1) personal growth, (2) purpose in life, and (3) self-acceptance.

We can see in table 3.7 that in terms of the three subscales— personal growth, purpose in life, and self-acceptance, our sample is doing best in terms of personal growth, followed by purpose in life. Self-acceptance was also in the normal range for 63 percent of our sample, and this was the area where more of our sample was likely to struggle. A high proportion of our sample (75 percent or more) felt a strong purpose in life, which corresponds with our personal well-being scores noted above.

If we look at well-being by celibacy type, we can see that those who are celibate from all relationships are more likely to have a higher percentage falling in the lower range on self-acceptance and purpose in life, when compared to the other two groups (see table 3.8).

TABLE 3.7. OVERALL WELL-BEING

Subscales of Well-Being	Normal		Lower	
	n	Percent	n	Percent
Personal Growth	269	90.6	28	9.4
Purpose in Life	231	77.8	66	22.2
Self-Acceptance	186	62.6	111	37.4

While self-acceptance was below normal range for 37 percent of our sample, it is important to remember that depression levels of our sample were comparable to the general population (see table 3.1 where 8 percent were moderately depressed and 1 percent severely depressed). Our sample of celibate gay Christians appears to have similar psychological strengths as the general population. One notable area where we may want to suggest providing support is the area of self-acceptance, followed by the fostering of purpose in life.

TABLE 3.8. WELL-BEING BY CELIBACY TYPE

Subscales of Well-Being	Celibate from All		Celibate from Same Sex		Mixed-Orientation Marriages	
	Normal	Lower	Normal	Lower	Normal	Lower
	n (percent)	n (percent)	n (percent)	n (percent)	n (percent)	n (percent)
Personal Growth	57 (87.7)	8 (12.3)	154 (92.2)	13 (7.8)	58 (89.2)	7 (10.8)
Purpose in Life	48 (73.8)	17 (26.2)	129 (77.2)	38 (22.8)	54 (83.1)	11 (16.9)
Self-Acceptance	34 (52.3)[a]	31 (47.7)	104 (62.3)	63 (37.7)	48 (73.8)[a]	17 (26.2)

Note[a]: Statistically significant group differences with $p \leq .05$

These areas—self-acceptance and purpose in life—need to remain a key focus of friends, family, and those providing ministry to celibate gay Christians.

We ran some additional analyses to explore the relationship between religiosity and psychological health. In doing this, we were able to distinguish between participants who were high and low on religiosity, and we looked at how these differences were related to their psychological health. We found that some religious practices, such as regular church attendance (once a week or more) and regular prayer (daily or more than once a week), were related to higher scores on well-being in general (life as a whole), and in particular in areas like personal relationships and feeling part of one's community, among other areas. To put this simply: attending church and engaging in other spiritual disciplines appear to help one's quality of life. Among those who are depressed or anxious, admittedly a small number of those in our study, they are already engaging in religious activities, such as attending church and spending time in prayer. Simply telling them to do more will likely not be helpful.

ATTACHMENT STYLES

In the past few years, we have begun studying the attachment style of celibate gay Christians. The classification of attachment styles began with John Bowlby, a British psychoanalyst who in the mid-to late twentieth century studied parent-child relationships and how they reflected different experiences of attachment vis-à-vis qualities such as support, care, and protection. Psychologist Mary Ainsworth extended these ideas and developed a taxonomy of responses associated with attachment. Other theorists and researchers have proposed how these attachment patterns can be present in adulthood. The theory of attachment that has developed over time can be illustrated along two axes: one axis reflecting avoidance (low to high) and one reflecting anxiety (low to high).[26] A person could have a *secure* attachment that would be characterized by both low avoidance of intimacy and low anxiety about intimacy and relationships. Another person could be low on avoidance but high on anxiety, thus reflecting what is called a *preoccupied* attachment. Still another person could be high on avoidance and low on anxiety (therefore *dismissive-avoidant*, distancing themselves from others) or high on avoidance and high on anxiety (therefore *fearful-avoidant*, ambivalent about closeness with others).

In some of our preliminary research with 118 celibate gay Christians[27] and 225 celibate gay Christians,[28] we looked at the prevalence of these four attachment styles (secure, preoccupied, fearful-avoidant, and dismissive-avoidant) as well as measuring their personal well-being (level of life satisfaction), the prevalence of distress (level of depression, anxiety, and distress), and intrinsic and extrinsic religiosity (the frequency of organized and nonorganized religious activity).

In many respects, our findings were very similar to what we reported previously. We found that celibate gay Christians experienced moderate to high well-being and mostly nonclinical levels of depression, anxiety, and stress. We also found that celibate gay Christians rated high in both organized (e.g., attending church) and non-organized (studying the Bible) religious practices, as well as high in intrinsic religiosity (meaning that religion matters in all aspects of their lives).

FIGURE 1. FOUR ATTACHMENT STYLES BASED UPON ANXIETY AND AVOIDANCE

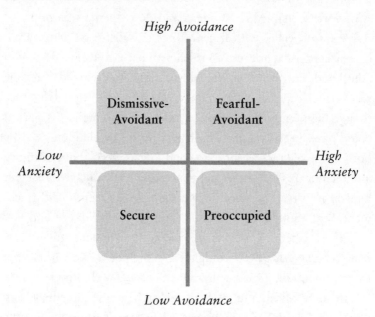

High Avoidance

Dismissive-Avoidant

Fearful-Avoidant

Low Anxiety

High Anxiety

Secure

Preoccupied

Low Avoidance

With regard to attachment styles, we found in our previous research that celibate gay Christians primarily have a *preoccupied* attachment style: that is, they rank low on avoidance and high on anxiety. The second most common attachment style we found was a *secure* attachment style, one low on both avoidance and anxiety.[29] Interestingly, attachment style was a significant predictor of the level of distress our participants experience. Those with a secure attachment style had lower scores of depression and anxiety than those with a preoccupied or fearful-avoidant style. Also, extrinsic and intrinsic spirituality had a significant positive relationship with levels of well-being: those with higher degrees of spiritual interest were more likely to report high personal well-being.

As we look at our sample of three hundred celibate gay Christians, we find very similar results. Our sample was most likely to report a *preoccupied* attachment style—41 percent of participants scored as having this style. Low on avoidance and high on anxiety, these participants want intimacy and pursue relationships, but they can easily become anxious and worry about their relationships, especially if the other person in the relationship is not as responsive as they feel they need. Those with a preoccupied attachment style often also hold a lower, more negative view of themselves.

The next most common attachment style among our sample was *secure* (28 percent), followed closely by *fearful-avoidant* (23 percent). When people have a *secure* attachment style, they are low on avoidance and low on anxiety, meaning that they tend to seek out intimacy and pursue relationships, and they are not particularly anxious about those relationships. They can regulate their emotions and tend to feel pretty comfortable with others as well as when they are by themselves.

Those who are fearful-avoidant in their attachment style tend to be rather ambivalent about closer, more intimate relationships. High in both anxiety and avoidance, they are not as comfortable with intimacy and tend not to pursue relationships. They may have a lower, more negative view of themselves.

How should we think about attachment styles? Attachment styles speak to past experiences in relationships with attachment figures. Based on the nature and quality of relationship to attachment figures, a person will have an attachment system that, later in life, can get activated: "Every event perceived as threatening by a person of any age tends to activate the attachment system."[30] When we talk of activating the attachment system, we are thinking of how perceived threats "automatically heighten access to attachment-related thoughts, feelings, and action tendencies."[31]

What we can expect to see are more interactional components of insecure and secure attachment processes. For securely attached people, threats can actually increase thoughts and memories about positive interactions with attachment figures in the past. In contrast, for insecurely attached people, threats increase access to negative thoughts and memories. Secure people are then primed to be confident in the effectiveness of available and responsive attachment figures, making approach (rather than avoidance) the most likely behavioral response. They tend to "lean into" others and have greater confidence that others will be there. Insecure people, on the other hand, are primed to be less confident in their unavailable or unresponsive attachment figures, leading to either hyperactivation or hypoactivation/deactivation to manage the fear. Attachment activation actually reminds insecure persons of noxious experiences in the past when affectional and safety needs were left unmet by persons who were considered attachment figures.[32]

In a large sample of celibate gay Christians, we expected to find some percentage reflecting each of the four adult attachment styles, as we did. So how does our sample of celibate gay Christians compare to the general population in terms of attachment styles? In a 1997 national study of eight thousand people, the most common attachment style was a secure attachment style, represented by 59 percent of respondents;[33] by comparison, 28 percent of our sample reported a secure attachment style. A total 25 percent of the national study participants reported either dismissive-avoidant or fearful-avoidant attachment styles,[34] which is slightly less common than the 31 percent we reported. Perhaps most notably, only 11 percent of those in the national study had a preoccupied type of attachment, which is much less common than the 41 percent we reported. On the whole, the celibate gay Christians we studied displayed comparable levels of avoidance but higher levels of anxiety than their counterparts in the national study, resulting in lower rates of secure attachment and higher rates of preoccupied attachment than are found in the general population.

FIGURE 2. FOUR ATTACHMENT STYLES BASED UPON ANXIETY AND AVOIDANCE

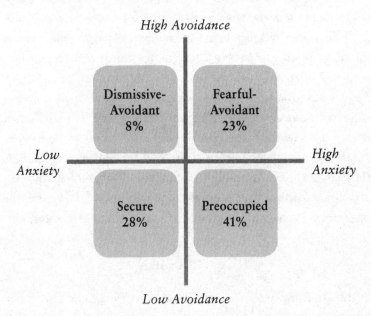

In follow-up analyses, we found that of those participants (n = 27) who have moderate or severe depression, two-thirds had a fearful-avoidant attachment style, followed by 22 percent with a preoccupied attachment pattern. Similarly, of those participants who have moderate or severe anxiety (n = 13), 62 percent had a fearful-avoidant attachment style and 38 percent preoccupied. No one who had a secure attachment style suffered from moderate or severe depression or anxiety.

Our sample, then, is much more likely than the general population to want to be close to people, but at the same time, they tend to worry about what others think about them and they worry about those who are closest to them. Other people may find them "clingy" or "high maintenance," and they perhaps need more encouragement or validation in their friendships. They may struggle with their sense of self-worth, further increasing their concern that others will not think highly of them.

It is important to remember, however, that these attachment patterns are not dispositional; rather, when we talk about attachment patterns we are talking about interactional patterns—how people interact in terms of having a fear-management system that gets activated when a person perceives a threat, feels fear, or just needs a safe haven or a secure base.[35] A person who has a more preoccupied attachment pattern rarely turns that off, and they see limited options for expanding their relationship resources because they are highly invested in maintaining the primary attachment relationships they have. Underestimating the importance of the few primary attachment people that person has would be a mistake, for the person will put a lot of energy into maintaining those relationships.

CONCLUSION

In this chapter, we related our findings on celibate gay Christians' attitudes about same-sex sexuality, same-sex behavior, causation (of sexual orientation), and whether orientation can change. We then considered whether it is healthy to live a celibate life. We realize that people's answers to this question are usually based on assumptions about sexuality and the role of sexual expression and intimacy in the life of an individual. We tried instead to provide an empirical answer to what we see as an empirical question. We were pleasantly surprised to report that celibate gay Christians are doing as well as they are on various measures of depression, anxiety, stress, and well-being. This was generally true even in cases in which those in mixed-orientation marriages appeared to pull the average scores "up" for the group.

Of course, the fact that many celibate gay Christians are doing better than we might have expected does not negate the challenges of those who are struggling. Diversity can be found among the experiences of celibate gay Christians, just as it can be found in the experiences of the general population. At the same time, it is clear from our research that celibate gay Christians are not all necessarily bound to emotionally unhealthy lives by virtue of their celibacy. These findings can inform our discussion of how best to respond to celibate gay Christians both at an individual level (person to person) and at a corporate level (in the church), as we will discuss later.

FOR DISCUSSION

1. Which response to the attitudinal statements (statements about causation, change, and the morality of same-sex behavior and relationships) surprised you most?
2. If someone asked you whether it is ever possible for a person to be celibate and emotionally healthy, how would you answer based on the findings presented in this chapter?
3. How would you describe a preoccupied attachment style? How could you help a friend who expresses this style?
4. What kind of support do you think a church community could provide to a celibate gay person who struggles with self-acceptance and purpose in life? What kind of messages would be helpful to foster in the church culture for these people?

CHAPTER 4

CELIBATE GAY CHRISTIANS' MILESTONE EVENTS

People do not wake up one morning and discover they are gay. The creation of sexual identity—a person's decision to use sexual identity labels, such as gay, to describe their sexual preference—is considered a developmental process. Most scholars of LGBTQ+ sexual identity development believe that people conclude they are gay (or lesbian or bisexual) through a series of experiences that can be thought of as milestone events in the formation of a gay (or lesbian or bisexual) identity.

Those who study sexual identity development used to focus on *stages* of identity formation. A person was thought to progress through a series of stages, moving predictably from an initial stage of awareness to a final stage of synthesis. The problem with stage models is that they presume everyone will pass through the same stages in a linear fashion. However, recent research suggests that sexual identity development is more nuanced and idiosyncratic than stage models can reflect. Scholarship on sexual identity development is moving away from a stage model approach and toward an approach that emphasizes specific events commonly associated with the formation of sexual identity. These specific events, referred to as *milestone events*, may not all be experienced by every person who identifies as gay, lesbian, or bisexual—nor will they necessarily be experienced in the same sequence by everyone—but they have proven to be significant in many people's journeys of sexual identity formation. Just as someone hiking a long trail will find and follow milestones along their journey, the person navigating sexual identity development is thought to find and follow a series of milestones.

To identify milestones that are significant in sexual identity development, researchers have interviewed and surveyed lesbian, gay, and bisexual adults about their experiences when they were younger. Some of the common milestone events they have identified are a person's first awareness of same-sex sexuality, which typically occurs following puberty; their decision to disclose their same-sex sexuality to another person, often called "coming out"; and their adoption of a private or public sexual identity label, such as "gay."

Savin-Williams and Cohen reported great diversity among the experiences of sexual minorities but still noted this common trend: "Most homoerotic youth recall same-sex attractions, fantasies, and arousal several years—on average—before questioning the meaning of these feelings."[1] Dube and Savin-Williams, in their study of white, black, Asian, and Latino male adolescents, reported the average age range at which these adolescents experienced milestones like awareness of same-sex attraction (ages eight to eleven), first same-sex behavior (ages twelve to fifteen), use of sexual identity labels for themselves (ages fifteen to eighteen), disclosure of identity to others (ages seventeen to nineteen), and first same-sex relationship (ages eighteen to twenty).[2] Although most of these milestones remain as significant as ever, the commitment to an identity label may be diminishing among sexual minority youth. Some youth prefer not to label themselves or may be open to a number of identity label options over time.[3]

Savin-Williams and Diamond[4] have also reported the average ages of common milestone events in another study of gay young adults. These included a remarkably early awareness of same-sex attractions (between ages seven and nine, which the researchers noted is likely an artifact of the way they worded the question and not typical for recalling first awareness of attractions), first behavior to orgasm (between ages fourteen and seventeen), first labeling of themselves as gay or lesbian (between ages sixteen and eighteen), and first disclosure of their sexual identity as gay or lesbian to others (at about age seventeen or eighteen).

Some milestone events mark first experiences of sexual behaviors, such as romantic kissing, fondling, and sexual behavior to orgasm. Other milestones mark psychological processes involved in identity formation as a gay person, such as meaning making that occurs when people first attribute their attraction to an emerging sense of identity. The distinction between behavior milestones and psychological ones is in some ways artificial; after all, behavior is a reflection of psychological experiences, and behavior also reinforces ways of thinking about oneself and one's identity. Also, some milestones are equally behavioral and psychological: a person's first same-sex sexual relationship, for instance, involves both repeated sexual behavior and the labeling of the relationship as a relationship.

In our previous work, we compared Christian sexual minorities who identified as gay with those who disidentified from a gay identity. By "disidentify," we mean that they chose not to identify with the broader LGBTQ+ community and did not consider themselves to be gay.[5] While both groups still experienced attraction to the same sex, we reported that Christians who disidentified with a gay identity were less likely than those who currently identified as gay to attribute their same-sex attractions to an intrinsic gay identity. Instead, they attributed their attractions to an external cause: the fall in Genesis 3, for example, or a faulty parent-child relationship. Both groups dealt with complexities as they sorted out their sexual identities: those who identified as gay did not settle into this identity until an average age of twenty-six, and those who disidentified from a gay identity settled into this disidentification at an average age of thirty-four.

We saw similar ambivalence among Christian sexual minorities toward the use of identity labels in our previous research on sexual minorities at Christian colleges and universities. In our first study, published in 2009, only 30 percent of sexual minority students attributed their attractions to a possible gay identity, and only 14 percent labeled themselves gay.[6] In a second study published four years later, 18 percent of sexual minorities attributed their attractions to a gay identity, and only 11 percent labeled themselves gay.[7] The percentage of sexual minority students who identified as gay increased in our most recent study of sexual minorities on Christian college campuses. In that study, 74 percent identified themselves as gay privately (to themselves), and 40 percent publicly identified as gay.[8]

Among the three hundred celibate gay Christians we surveyed for this study, most are not publicly known as gay. Even though most (76 percent) think of themselves as gay, most (57 percent) are not known to others as gay (see table 4.1). We saw a similar dynamic with our most recent college sample of sexual minorities.[9] Perhaps it is not a foregone conclusion that a public gay identity will be the inevitable consequence of sexual identity development and synthesis, but the reasons for not being publicly known as gay are unclear and may be a personal preference or for some may be related to how they believe those around them would respond to a public gay identity. We were curious if having a private but not public gay identity would be associated with mental health concerns, such as depression or anxiety. In our sample, there was no difference in depression or anxiety based on having a public sexual identity versus having only a private sexual identity as gay.

TABLE 4.1. MILESTONE EVENTS IN SEXUAL IDENTITY DEVELOPMENT

Milestone Event	Average Age (Standard Deviation)	n	Percentage
Initial confusion	13.0 (4.8)	264	88.0
Awareness of same-sex attraction	13.5 (5.8)	294	98.0
Fondled by same sex without orgasm	18.0 (8.5)	138	46.0
Initial attribution	19.0 (6.6)	260	86.7
Fondled by same sex to orgasm	21.0 (7.4)	99	33.0
Same-sex sexual behavior to orgasm	21.0 (7.1)	100	33.3
Private identity as gay	21.0 (8.7)	228	76.0
Disclosure	21.0 (6.8)	280	93.3
Romantically kissed by same sex	22.0 (8.1)	117	39.0
Public identity as gay	25.0 (9.2)	128	42.7

In our survey, we asked celibate gay Christians if they had experienced the milestones common to the sexual identity development of other LGBTQ+ individuals, and if so, at what age they experienced these milestones. We did not conduct interviews around each milestone event, but some milestone events did come up in our interviews, and what we learned corresponded with what we saw in our survey. Some of our interviewees also discussed additional experiences, such as the decision to be celibate and the use of the phrase "celibate gay Christian" as milestones in their sexual identity development. These additional milestones, because they are relatively unique to the celibate gay Christian experience of sexual identity development, also merit consideration.

Initial Confusion and Awareness of One's Same-Sex Attractions

Two of the earliest milestone events commonly experienced by people who later identify as gay are (1) awareness of their same-sex attractions and (2) feelings of confusion about their same-sex attractions. With regard to these two milestones, our sample of celibate gay Christians is quite similar to the broader community of gay and lesbian sexual minorities. Among our sample of celibate gay Christians, nearly all (98 percent) reported experiencing a first awareness of same-sex attractions, and most (88 percent) reported feelings of confusion about those attractions. This awareness and confusion usually occurred at roughly the same age, about thirteen years old on average.

Our celibate gay Christians answered differently when asked about the onset of their same-sex *feelings* than when asked about the onset of their same-sex *attractions*. For the most part, as we have just said, initial awareness of same-sex *attractions* occurred during, or just following, puberty. However, 98 percent of our sample reported earlier memories of same-sex *feelings*, at an average age of twelve. This suggests, perhaps, that these respondents experienced an *emotional draw* toward a person or people of the same sex even before developing a subsequent *sexual attraction* toward the same sex during or after puberty.

Knowing the precise nature of this emotional draw is difficult, if that is indeed the experience people are referring to when they discuss having prepubescent same-sex feelings. Some people report being aware of attraction to—or perhaps fascination with—the same sex as a child. We must remember, too, that people may assign retrospective meaning to their childhood memories as they reflect back on those memories through the lens of their current experience of same-sex sexuality. For example, Liam, a twenty-seven-year-old Caucasian celibate man, reflected on an early nonsexual interest in men that he would later come to understand as part of his same-sex sexuality: "I didn't really know what it was. As early as age seven, I was starting to have hints. The way I would describe it is, I would have these moments where I was looking at a guy or a picture of a guy and be like 'whoa.' And [I was] wondering what the rest of it looked like, or being sort of captivated."

Whereas nonsexual feelings like these may occur well before puberty, it is more common for gay and lesbian persons to report their first awareness of same-sex attraction at a later age, during or just following puberty. In our sample, as we noted above, 98 percent reported first developing same-sex attraction at an average age of thirteen.

How did our interviewees describe this milestone event as it contributed to their eventual self-understanding of sexual identity? Liam offered the following account of his own awareness of his same-sex sexuality and his eventual addiction to same-sex pornography:

> When I was thirteen, oh dear. Basically, well, in fact, what happened, it was one of the most awkward gay realizations I can imagine. What happened was, it was the middle of the night, and I snuck down to use the computer when I knew nobody else would be on it, and I searched for naked men. It wasn't until I did that that I had articulated to myself that I wanted to see that. So, I sort of came out to myself and [eventually] got addicted to porn.

Another interviewee, Charles, found himself comparing his newfound same-sex attractions to his adolescent friends' newfound opposite-sex attractions: "I would not say that things started to kind of crystallize maybe until I was in middle school, and I actually began to realize that, okay, I feel very strong attractions to certain guys in my school. And the kind of language that other guys were using to explain how they were talking about girls, that kind of described in some ways how I felt about these guys that I found very interesting."

Charles elaborated a little later in the interview: "I think it was more arresting in what would have been in like seventh or eighth grade when I went through puberty. So later then, of course, the sexual impulses, the sexual attractions, and all that kind of always had to do with other guys in my head and not other girls. . . . I remember in eighth grade clearly, really being like, *Oh, I think I am gay.*

Here Charles moved from an initial awareness of the sexual impulses and attractions associated with same-sex sexuality and into initial attributions, or meaning-making, about his experiences. In other words, he needed to make sense of his attractions, and his attractions needed to have a meaning assigned to them.

Lucas, a thirty-nine-year-old Caucasian male, also discussed his shift from a first awareness of same-sex attraction into meaning-making attributions:

> I think I was fifteen when I first experienced attractions I recognized as wanting to have sex with another man. I didn't have a similar desire to have sex with a woman. The meaning I attributed to it was that I was gay. . . . But on the other hand, when I was fifteen I thought that I would have to keep this completely secret, so it was something that [I] was much more trying to hide and run away from when I was fifteen, whereas now I can acknowledge it pretty comfortably, but it seems much less important than it was when I was fifteen.

Similarly, Ben, a twenty-four-year-old Caucasian male, felt the impulse to assign meaning to his experiences even though he lacked a label for them. He said, "There was always some kind of attraction or draw, so around eleven or twelve I started developing a broader curiosity. Around that time, I was really sad that I didn't have a good label. I knew I was different but didn't have the words to describe how I felt."

As we have seen from these interviews, attributions are closely related to people's initial awareness of attractions and their corresponding confusion about those attractions. Attributions have to do with meaning making—how a person makes sense of their attractions. The meaning people assign can be tied to the etiology, or causes, of same-sex sexuality. The meaning may also be tied to more existential, including religious, forms of meaning.

Attributions: Etiological and Existential

Most of our sample of celibate gay Christians recalled attributing their same-sex attractions to a gay identity. That is, they processed their attractions as signaling that they were predominantly oriented in their romantic attractions toward the same sex. Once they had concluded that they were gay, they often subsequently wrestled with the existential reasons for their orientation, performing a second attributional search for meaning by asking, "Why am I gay?" We will return to this question in a moment. First, however, let's consider the etiological meaning that celibate gay Christians attributed to their attractions.

Ben said, "For me, it wasn't probably until I was fourteen or fifteen that I experienced I was gay. It was shameful. . . . At that time, I . . . adamantly denied that and I said, 'No, no, of course not' . . . but oddly enough, that was kind of also the time that I can remember, *Oh my gosh, that is maybe the word that applies to what I [am] experiencing.*"

Later in the interview, Ben shared his choice not to obsess over the causes of his orientation: "I didn't have to try and figure out some dirt with my relationship with my dad or anything like that in order to justify having the experiences that I had. That for whatever reason I am attracted to other guys rather than other girls, whether that was biological, nurture, nature, whatever. It just was."

Charles also grappled with theories of causation. Unlike Ben, he found them helpful to consider, and he believed that more than one of the theories illuminated his own experience: "Like it is some combination of I was born that way, people did things to each other and to me, and I also made my own choices; it's a combination of all of those things, and the exact proportion that is in that cocktail I'm not quite sure." Charles seems to draw from a working theory of causation in which multiple influences contributed to the development of his same-sex sexuality.

Once people had reached the conclusion that they were gay and considered the etiology of their sexuality, they sometimes went on to consider existential or religious attributions for the meaning and purpose of their sexuality. For example, Eugene shared the following belief about the existential meaning of his orientation: "I think that my sexual orientation is [God's] gift to me. There is in Catholic spirituality the idea of a charism, a gift that God gives individuals. . . . I believe that homosexuality has a charismatic aspect to it." Though Eugene believes his same-sex orientation should be expressed through celibacy, he still attributes the orientation itself to God's generosity. Others we interviewed noted the way they believed sin and the fall had impacted their experience of sexual desire. Patrick, a twenty-seven-year-old Caucasian celibate man, said, "If you mean where does [my same-sex attraction] come from, I would say it's attributed to the fall, when things got mixed up. I don't think there is anything wrong with seeing the beauty in other men. It seems to be commoner for gay men to do that than straight men. But in and of itself that's an art rather than a sin."

Lucas also discussed the complex relationship of the fall to his orientation: "Part of how I see those attractions in relation to my faith is that there are lustful attractions that are part of the fall, but also part of it is healthy desires for friendship that are not in themselves sinful or temptation but have to be guided in the right way toward healthy friendship rather than toward sexual desire."

For Lucas, the fall was one of the causes to which he attributed his same-sex sexuality, but this alone did not exhaust his understanding of what it means to be gay. He also referred to "healthy desires for friendship," suggesting that a gay orientation has constructive as well as sinful components.

Alex offered a reflection on celibacy as a high calling, interpreting his same-sex sexuality with an attribution that ascribes spiritual meaning and significance to it:

> Celibacy is . . . a vocation; it is a calling by God. I've never quite understood the argument that Christian gay people have celibacy forced on them. I think God calls us to things without our permission. Straight people who become celibate generally do so because [of] God. . . . Divorced people have to remain celibate. . . . I am strongly for the position that celibacy is a calling . . . more specifically, it's a calling to not be married, to remain in [an] unmarried state, and also to abstain from genital sexual behavior.

Of Course I Wasn't Gay
Bridget Eileen

The first time I ever realized I was "different," I was standing dumbstruck in the middle of the shoe department of a retail store. I was only four years old, so my awareness of being "different" was not so much a conscious thing as it was felt. Mom had taken me out shopping for a new pair of shoes. But every last pair that she paraded before me fell flat. I didn't like any of them, and my eyes began to wander the store.

Finally, I spotted them. Only a few aisles away. And they were exactly what I wanted! I abruptly dashed off, calling out to my mother that I'd found them! A few seconds later, I was clutching a pair of brown loafers in my hand and sizing them up against my feet. They were perfect.

And then my mom delivered the news.

"Honey, you can't get these."

I looked at her dumbfounded. Why not? They fit me, see?

"These are boy shoes," she said with all the patience of a mother who really does truly care, "and you can't get shoes from the boys' section, honey. You're a little girl."

Objections came to my lips in a variety of four-year-old whines that essentially amounted to, "But I want them!!!" Not prone to tantrums, however, I eventually dropped my complaints and watched in disbelief as my mother placed the only pair of shoes in the entire store that I wanted back on the shelf, leading me away from what I now understood to be the "boys'" section. Silent tears were the only sign of my disappointment.

Such was my life growing up in the 1990s, struggling to make sense of my tastes and preferences. I hated Sundays more than anything because I had to wear dresses and keep my hair down with cute little bows at the top. During the week, when I got out of school, I raided my brother's old clothes and tied up my hair in a ponytail to keep its annoying length out of the way.

Rarely did I ever consider that my tastes were "masculine" until people kindly enlightened me. I never felt like a boy. I was definitely a girl, but other girls would whisper behind my back, "Ew, doesn't she look like a boy?" And a well-meaning friend of my parents even told me in private when

I was fourteen that he had been getting concerned about my "masculine" appearance.

I was definitely a girl, but I was attracted to things that "only boys" liked. And that extended to people. Boys were so much easier to be friends with. Girls were confusing and weird. I didn't get them. And as I entered puberty, they only became more confusing. But also alluring. Beautiful. Intoxicating.

My first crush never struck me as a crush. I thought about her and dreamed about her and wrote about her in my journal. But like everything else in my life, I never thought that my experience was "abnormal." Yet somehow I knew that I should keep my feelings to myself. I thought maybe every girl was feeling what I felt and just kept it a secret too. But the more I talked to girls, the more I realized that I was different; and as I entered college, I began to wonder if something was wrong.

Then one day a friend "turned me on."

I agonized over what happened for days, and for the next several years I thanked God that I was a Christian, otherwise I'd be gay. What a relief! Of course I wasn't gay. Christians weren't gay. I wasn't gay. My likes and dislikes weren't gay. Just like my attractions weren't gay. Just like my first kiss wasn't gay. Just like . . . well, eventually my reasoning broke down.

I knew I was gay, but I couldn't admit it. According to everything I'd ever been taught, you could be either Christian or gay. But you couldn't be both. If I was a Christian, I was safe. But if I was gay, well . . .

Thoughts of burning in hell created a darkness that swirled in my head like poison until I awoke one night in a panic, convinced that God would strike me dead and send me to eternal damnation at any moment. Not being able to fall back asleep, I did the only thing I could think of doing: I prayed a prayer of desperation to a God that terrified me.

Gently, in the early morning darkness, something prompted me to turn to Romans 8 as I prayed. "Who shall separate us from the love of Christ?" (v. 35)—I whispered the words like they were my last, and a gospel truth quietly arose like the dawn upon my soul: that God loves gay people too.

It's an obvious truth, but you just don't hear it in church. So I had to hear it from the Bible instead. So what if I was gay? So what if I was different? Christ didn't change from one person to the next. And in the months that followed, I read God's Word, knowing for the first time that it really did contain truth for all people, including different people. Including gay people.

And that meant that God's story of redemption included me, gay as I ever was.

Sexual Behavior/Experimentation

Because of their religious convictions, many celibate gay Christians never experience the same-sex sexual behaviors that serve as milestones of sexual identity development for other gay, lesbian, and bisexual individuals. For example, only one-third of those we surveyed had engaged in sexual behavior to orgasm with a member of the same sex. Less than half had been fondled (46 percent) or romantically kissed (39 percent) by someone of the same sex.

Those who did experience these milestones in their sexual identity development often felt deep guilt or regret about them because of their beliefs about sexual ethics. Noel shared the following about milestones in his life: "I explored a few times in middle school and junior high with someone, but that wasn't really a relationship; that was pure experimentation. Which was, you know, guilt-wracking."

Disclosure

Coming out as gay—what we are referring to as disclosure—is an important milestone event for most LGBTQ+ persons. Given the tensions that exist for celibate gay Christians in the church today, disclosure can be relationally devastating, which is perhaps part of the reason that so many celibate gay Christians who identify as gay privately do not do so publicly. This reluctance to disclose was captured in our interview with Ben, who shared about the tensions that exist until another person knows about his same-sex sexuality: "Until somebody knows . . . no matter how much they know about me or love me . . . until they know this one thing, they might not [love me anymore]. This might be the deal breaker, end of our relationship up to that point."

Because of the stigma around being gay, another celibate gay Christian told us how he disclosed his sexuality to friends by describing it as "the worst thing" that could have happened to him:

I think I possibly disclosed to two friends when I was sixteen or seventeen. I think it was through an instant messaging application on the computer, like . . . "Hey, try to guess the worst thing that you possibly could think is going on with me." And they'd be like, "Cancer, or your mom is dying, your dad is dying," and I'd be like, "No, it's actually worse. I think I'm gay."

Disclosure is formative not only because it allows the celibate gay person to be known by others but also because it creates the possibility for them to experience acceptance and even to hear stories similar to their own. Geoff, a twenty-four-year-old Caucasian celibate man, told about the following milestone in his life: "I kind of had him read a letter I had written. After reading it he told me that he, too, struggled with same-sex attraction, which was kind of this huge, huge thought for me in my story, going from like total isolation to, *Oh my gosh, the first kind of peer I share this with acknowledges and understands this*."

Gay as Sexual Identity Label

Another milestone for many celibate gay Christians was beginning to identify themselves as gay. Lucas explained his choice of terminology: "I had much more positive associations with *gay* than with *homosexual*, and I think for me *gay* had never had the connotation of embracing going to gay bars or whatever. It was just a description of my attractions, and it didn't seem that people who said really negative things about homosexuals would make that distinction."

Lucas shared further: "So *same-sex attracted* in some ways is an advance in clarity over *ex-gay*, but also it has an organizational history behind it . . . and it's a clumsy term that if I try to talk to most people, they would wonder why I wouldn't just say I was gay."

Charles arrived at the term *gay* earlier in his journey, and it felt to him like the obvious word for someone experiencing attraction to the same sex: "I remember in eighth grade clearly, really being like, *Oh, I think I am gay.*" Ben explained that he initially resisted calling himself gay because he still hoped to escape his same-sex attractions: "Gay became what identified those people, the other people, the people who had given up. . . . For me, I was same-sex attracted, things like that."

OPPOSITE-SEX BEHAVIORS AND RELATIONSHIPS

Despite the previous assumption that sexual orientation is an immutable characteristic in all persons, recent research has documented shifts in sexual behavior, sexual identity labels, and other aspects of sexuality. This has been true for sexual minority females[10] and males.[11] Of course, sexual minorities may pursue experiences with the opposite sex for a variety of reasons—to see, for example, if they have the capacity for a meaningful opposite-sex intimate relationship or, perhaps more frequently, to keep people from suspecting they are gay.

We asked our sample of three hundred celibate gay Christians about their experiences with the opposite sex in terms of attractions, behaviors, and relationships (see table 4.2). Fifty-three percent reported that they had been romantically kissed by someone of the opposite sex at an average age of eighteen. By comparison, in our most recent study of sexual minorities at Christian colleges and universities, 62 percent reported that they had been romantically kissed by someone of the opposite sex at an average age of sixteen.

TABLE 4.2. EXPERIENCES WITH OPPOSITE SEX BEHAVIORS AND RELATIONSHIPS

Milestone Event	Average Age (Standard Deviation)	n	Percentage
Romantically kissed by opposite sex	18.0 (5.5)	159	53.0
Opposite sex relationship	18.0 (6.0)	162	54.0
Fondled by opposite sex without orgasm	20.0 (7.1)	99	33.0
Fondled by opposite sex to orgasm	22.5 (5.7)	69	23.0
Sexual behavior with opposite sex	23.0 (5.9)	70	23.3

About 33 percent of our sample reported that they had been fondled by someone of the opposite sex (without achieving orgasm) at an average age of twenty. This behavior occurred both less frequently and later than what we encountered in our previous study,[12] where 46 percent reported that they had been fondled by someone of the opposite sex at an average age of sixteen.

In terms of sexual behavior to orgasm with the opposite sex, 23 percent of our sample reported such behavior, with an average age of nearly twenty-three. Again, this behavior happened both more frequently and earlier in our study of Christian college students: about one-third (32 percent) reported sexual behavior with someone of the opposite sex that led to orgasm, and this activity occurred at an average age of eighteen.[13]

ADDITIONAL MILESTONES

So far we have looked at how and when gay celibate Christians experience (or forgo) the common milestone events of sexual identity development shared by most gay, lesbian, and bisexual individuals. In addition, we have considered that a subset of our sample has also had milestone experiences with opposite-sex behaviors and relationships. In the final section of this chapter, we discuss additional milestones of sexual identity development that are in many ways unique to the experience of celibate gay Christians: the theological and terminological milestones that have led these individuals to consider themselves celibate gay Christians.

Grappling with Side A

Many of those who now identify as celibate gay Christians have been through a theological journey of sorts before arriving at their current view. One common milestone for celibate gay Christians is a season of encountering, grappling with, or perhaps even being temporarily convinced by Side A (affirming) theology. Not everyone we interviewed has had experiences with Side A theology, but a number of our interviewees did have formative interactions with this view. For example, Lucas said, "During that period, I was certainly spending a lot of time dreaming about the future, so there was a sense in which a lot of what I wanted to become in my later teens—there was definitely a Side A element in that. The desire to have a romantic relationship did not end when I became Side B, but I just had more of a reason to resist it."

Lucas went on to tell how he engaged with Scripture:

> Reading the Bible in my later teens, when I started sorting things out more clearly and realizing that even though the conservative stuff I'd seen was hateful and ungracious, it was hard to get Side A reading out of the Bible. So, if I wanted to take the Bible seriously, it was hard to see how I could reconcile that with being in a gay relationship. . . . I think as far as my beliefs go, [Side A theology] creates more difficulties and brings up a lot more reasons for dissonance, but none of those affirming theologies have changed my interpretation of the Bible or given me a sort of fundamental doubt that that's the way I need to go.

Eugene disclosed the following about milestones in his life:

> I'll be really honest, I really wanted for Side A to be true. I always wanted that, for [a same-sex relationship] to be something I can pursue. At the same time, I just couldn't find enough explanation for the theology, and I know they say it's biological or whatever—I mean, I get that part. Just the fact that it couldn't convince me to go outside of my values, or just my traditional beliefs. I honestly—traditional values can very easily be logically explained away. There were times that I wanted to just walk out on Side B, but there never was enough evidence on the Side A where I really wanted to be.

Eugene was not the only interviewee who spoke of a deep desire to shift to a Side A theology and pursue a relationship. Xavier, a Caucasian celibate gay man, said the following about grappling with Side A theology: "I tried very hard to persuade myself with Side A theology, and that was because I was completely fed up, I was exhausted with the effort of trying to be celibate, I couldn't see the point, and I just wanted to be done." Despite his desire to shift theologically, however, Xavier found himself unpersuaded by Side A.

Grappling with Side X

In addition to wrestling with Side A theology, many of those we interviewed also wrestled with the question of whether they could change their sexual orientation. Again, not all celibate gay Christians experience this milestone, but many find that their sexual identity development is influenced by a period of believing that God intends to remove their attractions for the same sex and seeking out this transformation. Again, this attitude is sometimes referred to as "Side X," the X standing for "ex-gay."

For example, Charles reported that his shift toward the celibate gay Christian camp was influenced in part by his changing perspective toward orientation change: "I think I also saw that orientation change, in a way, had been an idol for me. It's like worshipping this idea of being a 'normal Christian,' 'normal' being getting married and having kids in the Sunday school."

Sebastian, a thirty-two-year-old Caucasian male, offered the following:

> I was talking to this friend. He asked me probably one of the most sane questions I've ever been asked. The question he asked me was, "If God doesn't change your orientation, will you still serve him?" And I said—I thought about it for a second, and I said, "Yeah." I think that's when I began to

entertain the notion of . . . that instead of being Side X or for reparative therapy or orientation change or ex-gay or whatever you want to call it—that's when I began to get through and go, *Okay, maybe there's a separation between my internal experience of temptation and what everyone else was calling, "Don't adopt a gay identity or act on those impulses or anything like that."* I think my becoming settled in sort of a Side B mind-set would probably be the fall of 2001. Even though nobody ever called it that then, of course, I think that's when I started to come to terms with those beliefs.

Aiden said,

And at least how I remember it, as much as I remember from when I was growing up, the reparative side never felt like it made sense with my experience. . . . I couldn't understand how God would transform someone, or it seemed like a much more remote thing than they would describe. At the same way, I couldn't find my way around biblical ideas allowing sexuality that would be in line with a more Side A position.

Landing on Side B

Regardless of how they have handled theological questions about Side A and Side X ministry considerations, all of the celibate gay Christians we surveyed have landed on a Side B theology. Charles explained how he discovered the possibility of an approach apart from the Side A and Side X approaches:

[Arriving at Side B rather than ex-gay] was through some friends who were part of Exodus but had been involved with the Gay Christian Network, where this sort of Side A and Side B terminology sort of originated. Which I had never had anything to do with, but they kind of explained that position.

In my mind, there were only two positions before: there was you either were gay and acting out on it, or you weren't and were trying to change. So, the third position, that there were people that were not acting out on it, that were following what the Lord was saying . . . that was a new decision for me. So, I guess I hadn't been aware that was an identity until 2011, but I felt that in many ways it captured my experience.

Lucas reflected on the transformative power of singleness and celibacy:

[I came to] that realization that there are benefits to being single and . . . [that I am still] able to serve God. So, when Paul talks about marriage and celibacy in 1 Corinthians 7, he is saying to be content with where you are, to not seek marriage, and so it seems to me unwise to desperately place myself into a marriage where I wasn't that attracted [to my spouse] when celibacy was also an option.

Lucas elaborated further:

The other thing [that helped me arrive at a Side B position] was a close friend. That relationship was . . . we were on the borderline between friendship and romance, though there was never anything sexual in it, and with that friendship realizing that love is not the same thing as sex. Saying no to gay sex did not mean being completely isolated. It was possible to have close friendships that were not sexual.

Others we interviewed held much different perspectives before identifying themselves as celibate gay Christians. Sebastian discussed his journey from being repelled by his own same-sex sexuality to landing at a place of greater self-acceptance: "I saw my same-sex attraction as being something that was fundamentally noxious to God, as opposed to something that he accepted me in my brokenness and moved me on toward holiness." Sebastian explained the shift in his perspective by saying, "If I am going to understand my own sexual orientation, I have to have a robust theology of the fall. It seems to me the effects of the fall are more far-reaching than most people are willing to give them credit for." Speaking of his same-sex sexuality today, Sebastian offered, "It's not something that makes me sick to my stomach anymore. It's not something that's disgusting that I find guys attractive."

Sebastian was not the only celibate gay Christian we interviewed who had journeyed over time from disgust and self-hatred to a posture of hopeful optimism about his same-sex sexuality. Interviewee Charles commented, "But for me, the point of celibacy is not to not have sex; it is to find in the church what a married person would find in that one partner." For Charles, celibacy could be embraced as an opportunity: "And I think that if I find myself alone, [it is] because I don't have the courage enough to go into those places where people need community and are hungry and help provide it. So, yeah, lifelong celibacy is scary, but if I have the courage and if I have the creativity, it can actually be an extremely fulfilling life."

Charles's understanding of celibacy led him to approach it optimistically even when it felt like a form of suffering: "Actually, I think that the biggest benefit that any story of any Christian who suffers or who has struggles is that suffering isn't actually punishment from God, that suffering is actually often like a grace from God."

Even for those who chose to enthusiastically embrace celibacy, this did not mean that they stopped feeling drawn toward relationships. Ben said, "I began to fall for one particular guy . . . the guy who I thought I got along with just as friends . . . and so that really changed a lot. Celibacy for me became—it changed from *Oh, I could very easily be single for the rest of my life*, to *I am actually giving up something that feels very natural. It feels very normal.*"

Use of Celibate Gay Christian Designation

For some of those we interviewed, the use of the label "celibate gay Christian" functioned as a milestone. Of course, the meanings contained by the label had often already been marked by other theological and experiential milestones: that is, those who began calling themselves "celibate gay Christians" were usually already professing Christians, already aware of their same-sex sexuality, and already committed to celibacy prior to adopting the label. However, this terminological milestone tied each of these other threads together into a more coherent private—or, in some cases, public—sexual identity.

For example, Ben shared the following about this milestone in his life:

> Sometime around mid-to late junior year [of college] was when I read *Washed and Waiting* by Wesley Hill. And his kind of take on the whole thing very much fit my impression. And so I began to try to experiment more with using the label *gay*. . . . So maybe like senior year, depending on who I was sharing with, I began to switch labels from *same-sex attraction* to defining as a *celibate gay Christian*.

The decision to use *celibate gay Christian* as a label is an interesting one, and a recent one, at least in the Christian circles with which we are familiar.

CONCLUSION

People who privately or publicly identify as gay can look back on their lives and identify important milestone events that brought them to where they are today in terms of their sexual identity. Those of us who want to better understand the sexual identities of gay-identifying individuals will be better equipped to do so once we understand what these milestones are and the role they typically play in helping sexual minorities attribute meaning to their experiences and develop a robust sense of personhood. In this chapter, we discussed many common milestone events and evaluated the extent to which these experiences shaped how our sample of celibate gay Christians saw themselves.

Most of our sample began their journeys of sexual identity development with feelings of confusion about their same-sex attraction. As with other recent research of Christian sexual minorities,[14] most participants in this study initially attributed their same-sex feelings to a gay identity. Some milestones they encountered subsequently seem to have consolidated this sense of identity, solidifying its trajectory; other milestones reflected exploration, experimentation, and even resistance of the sexual identity or the theology of sexual ethics that they would finally come to accept. We looked in some detail at how people make meaning of their same-sex sexuality, including their initial attributions and their decision to adopt "celibate" and "gay" as important aspects of their sexual identity.

Milestone events are widely discussed in the literature on sexual identity formation. They reflect key experiences that are a part of a process of discovery of who a person is. For celibate gay Christians, some of these milestones place them in the broader LGBTQ+ community and provide them with a sense of shared experience. Other milestones, such as landing on a Side B rather than a Side A view of same-sex sexual behavior, place them at odds with the broader LGBTQ+ community. Landing on Side B rather than Side X places them at odds with some conservative churches and Christian leaders who hold that a person can expect to change their attractions if they try hard enough or have enough faith.

FOR DISCUSSION

1. Why do you think people who study sexual identity development describe several of the experiences we reviewed in this chapter as milestone events in the formation of sexual identity?

2. Which milestone events stand out to you as particularly salient to celibate gay Christians, and why would you say those events are so salient?

3. Which milestone events reported by celibate gay Christians put them at odds with the broader LGBTQ+ community? Which milestones provide celibate gay Christians with a sense of shared community with others who are LGBTQ+?

4. Which milestone events experienced by celibate gay Christians put them at odds with many local churches?

5. Although the theological or doctrinal debates about sexual behavior (Side A, Side B, Side X) are not commonly studied by mainstream researchers in LGBTQ+ studies of sexual identity formation, why do you think they were cited by so many celibate gay Christians in this project?

CHAPTER 5

REFLECTIONS *for the* CHURCH

We should always, in terms of society, we
should be saying, "Come here and really be
a community, and let's share in Christ's love,
and we're all broken, we are all broken, we
all struggle with different sins," so church
should be humble in that way, I think.

Eugene, a celibate gay Christian

Churches handle sexual identity and faith issues very differently. Even churches that share a traditional Christian sexual ethic may differ considerably in their approach to questions about the nature and morality of same-sex attraction, the use of sexual identity labels, and methods of ministering to and including those struggling with same-sex attraction or otherwise negotiating sexual identity and faith in the life of the church. As we have seen, not all of our sample is in agreement about how important it is to them to identify as celibate gay Christians, so we are bound to see diversity in individual preferences and in suitability of fit with individual churches. Rather than presuming to settle the issue of how churches should respond, then, we simply want to begin a conversation—a design plan that we can think through together. First, we want to listen to what pastors say they are looking for as they address sexual minority matters in their churches. Then we turn to what celibate gay Christians recommend. We also want to look at themes from related research that might enhance our understanding of how the church could approach sexual identity and faith, both inside the body of Christ and as a witness to the culture around it.

WHAT PASTORS ARE LOOKING FOR

In a study we conducted of seminary-educated pastors, we were surprised to learn how they processed sexual identity concerns, what they wanted to focus on, and what they thought was needed. It is not surprising, perhaps, to hear pastors frame sexual identity issues in terms of sin; however, we are concerned that relegating the whole category of gay identity to the realm of sin makes pastors ill equipped to address the nuances that arise when celibate gay Christians exist within or enter into their communities, especially in terms of identifying paths for pastoral care at both individual and communal levels.

We asked study participants what additional training would be helpful to them in the area of sexual identity. Interestingly, some participants pushed back against the idea of receiving any research-based training. Instead, they preferred to view all sexual identity issues as sin issues, and they considered it the mission of the church to treat all sin equally.[1] For example, one pastor explained his reluctance to invest resources in training on sexual identity:

> I believe that the causes [of same-sex sexuality] are largely beyond the control of the church and would be, therefore, a waste of training resources. Likewise, "treatment" of same-sex issues shouldn't differ too much from any struggle a believer may be having. How many specific recovery ministries

should a church have? Alcohol, drugs, sexual sin, consumerism, greed, pride, etc. It's all sin. . . . Improving "climate" seems vague, but I think it's closer to what is needed in most churches. An open embracing of purity as a value for all . . . , not just those with same-sex attraction.

This pastor's framing of sexual identity concerns in terms of "sin" is certainly not uncommon. However, this pastoral response seems ill equipped to respond to the celibate gay Christians we have seen in our study, a group of individuals who—while quite "conservative" in terms of their willingness to live out costly obedience to a traditional biblical sexual ethic—experience their sexual identity differently than most pastors.

Other pastors who deemphasized the importance of training did so not because they felt it was unimportant but because they preferred to refer sexual identity concerns to someone outside the church who could be a resource. They voiced a desire for trained professionals, typically from a faith background, to work with people in their churches experiencing same-sex attraction. For example, one pastor described his desire for outside help concisely: "Is 'treatment' the right word? If the option had been 'counseling,' I would have checked that option." In other words, for some pastors, a referral to a local counselor is a viable alternative to training. While we can appreciate the desire to expand one's referral network, that pastor and that church will still be the church home to a Christian who is looking to be a part of the life of that local faith community.

Still other pastors acknowledged that they and their fellow pastors would benefit from more training. Some of them felt the need for training at multiple levels, including better understanding of the causes of same-sex sexuality and greater wisdom for pastoral care: "I am not up on the most current research as to causes. I know little treatment other than reparative treatment or nonjudgmental treatment. I've not read anything on improving the youth ministry climate. I have participated in a conference and had family counseling regarding a response of grace and truth." For some pastors, improving pastoral care would be accompanied by training in good, practical theology: "I need to see a clear biblical response balanced with a program or ministry approach to help these individuals." Still others shared an interest in engaging the topic in a culturally sensitive way. Several pastors expressed a desire for help in bridging the historic gap between the church and the LGBTQ+ community in a manner consistent with their values. This tension was described by one pastor: "I think we condemn all aspects of LGBT lifestyle and behaviors when there could be much to gain from recognizing the pain and discrimination they suffer. But to do that in a meaningful and complete way requires more dynamic interaction with LBGT people where the church takes a learner's posture and asks genuine questions with a desire to learn to love."

Celibate gay Christians may find it helpful to understand what pastors are looking for and what they think is important in these discussions. At the same time, perhaps one way the church can learn, as this pastor desires to do, is to listen to the experiences of celibate gay Christians. We asked the celibate gay Christians we interviewed what changes they would recommend in their churches. Their responses follow.

WHAT CELIBATE GAY CHRISTIANS SAY IS NEEDED

The celibate gay Christians we interviewed offered several suggestions about what is needed in the church today. Their suggestions included listening, making stories more visible, vocalizing that celibate gay Christians are wanted and needed, and creating a healthy culture for singles.

Begin by Listening

A common theme we saw in our interviews was the recommendation that people begin by listening. For example, Lucas has this suggestion for churches and church leaders:

> [Church leaders should] learn to listen to the gay Christians that they encounter, because people have very different experiences. . . . I think one of the things that is a problem is that a lot of Christians don't know what the ordinary lives of sexual minorities are like. Just being willing to listen to what the different people's experience is and not to expect that once you've heard one person's experience you've heard them all. Also seeing them primarily as people created in God's image with challenges to overcome and then kind of working on a case-by-case basis the same way you would with anyone else. . . . [What] I would want to see is looking at people much more as individuals and evaluating their individual strengths and weaknesses [rather than] seeing them in the category of gay, bisexual, lesbian, whatever and trying to judge them by what you know about that category.

Similarly, Jean offered the following:

> I don't feel free to move forward talking about [sexual identity] because I still get the feeling that [church people] don't want to. They don't—they really just don't want to engage with it, they don't want to talk about it. They just think that the struggle with this is truly sinful. . . . I think there's a lot of people that get there but they still don't—they don't welcome conversation. It makes them uncomfortable. . . .
>
> I don't think you get more comfortable with something just by silence and leaving it—letting it lie. Like, that's the

default. That's the tendency, is just to not talk about it so it doesn't make you uncomfortable. And it would just take a lot of proactivity, but that needs to change, because I think it's all kind of on people that are dealing with it to be really vocal.

In other words, Jean is concerned that the burden of creating constructive dialogue about sexuality in the church is always placed on sexual minorities, while those who are comfortable with the status quo feel free to remain silent. She also offered the following suggestions for the church as she reflected on the willingness of celibate gay Christians to share from their experiences: "But there's a whole lot of people that are more willing to talk about it than you realize, if they sense that you're coming at it from a student perspective and not from the 'know-it-all.' I think you'll find that most people aren't gonna bite if you say the wrong thing—if you ask awkward questions or are utterly unprepared for the conversation."

Aiden shared his thoughts on how churches might be stretched to listen to and understand different experiences:

On the more conservative side, I mean, there's a thousand ways they can improve and try and help, even just having some experience of talking to other gay Christians who aren't the shining example types that pop up in the magazines or anything, but outside of the people they know at the altar, Christians who are very safe. I think they really need to reach outside of that and be open to not just hearing the positions other Christians come from, but really understanding where [LGBTQ+ individuals outside the church] are coming from, and not . . . talking to them feeling like you have to have a response to them. Really just being there to listen. That's one of the things the church really needs.

Vocalize That LGBTQ+ People Are Wanted and Needed

In addition to listening to LGBTQ+ people, our sample of celibate gay Christians felt that it was important for sexual-majority Christians to verbalize the value of sexual-minority people in the church. Jean gave the following suggestions for the church: "I think that people who have same-sex attraction and are considering celibacy, I think they need to hear the message that they are wanted and needed—that as church people and leaders in ministry, they shouldn't be automatically discounted due to their orientation."

Jean went on to say: "I think people think, *Okay, I can't get married.* . . . *For a man, I don't want to marry a woman, but I can't marry a man, and now I can't do church or ministry. I can't be used by God, because who would want me?* And I think that's a lie that needs to be beat down over time." Belonging in a church community, Jean suggests, doesn't just mean that people allow you to be present; it means being given opportunities to serve that community and become an irreplaceable part of it.

Make Stories Visible

In addition to listening to sexual minorities and vocalizing that they are wanted and needed, another key step in communicating their worth is to make them visible to those around them. One interviewee, Charles, reflected on the power of making celibate gay Christians' stories visible as they occupy positions of service and leadership:

> People need to see people who are open about their sexuality but are also open about the fact that they are not acting on it. They are choosing to believe that Christ is enough. That those people are visible in leadership positions in a way that people know about their story. That once people see that it's not that weird for a celibate gay Christian to be in a leadership

position, then there's nothing to rule them out. And I think that in and of itself becomes a powerful message.

Sebastian similarly emphasized the value of having gay celibate Christians serving publicly and visibly in the church:

I think that there should be people serving publicly that that's part of their story. I think that that congregation should be willing to hire them (if they are qualified, of course). . . . I think it would be helpful for people to see other people living transparent lives, whether they are in leadership or in the congregation, that gay doesn't mean promiscuous. Gay doesn't mean having sex at all necessarily. I think that would be really helpful for people to see.

Foregrounding the stories of celibate gay Christians is valuable not only because it increases people's awareness of sexual identity issues at an abstract level but also because it makes those issues tangible, enfleshing them in the lives of real people. When sexual minorities are visible and tangible in a church, church leaders and congregants can bring to mind actual people when conversation turns to sexuality. Instead of dealing abstractly with sexuality as a mere controversial issue, churches can sensitively address the lives of individuals, just as many churches have already learned to do with other controversial issues. Interviewee Lucas commented,

[With], for example, divorce and remarriage, or premarital sex, or even abortion, most pastors realize that when they talk about these issues . . . they have real faces in mind. They preach about it, but they also understand the human stories behind the issues they are preaching about, and I think that gives more of a tenderness to how they approach the issues. More effort to understand the people they are speaking with.

But I think, a lot of times, talk about homosexuality is very abstract rather than focused on trying to understand people who want to be "gay married." They talk about it in terms of much bigger societal things, and also . . . fearfully, as in, "Those people out there are out to get us." So I think the main thing in terms of approaching the culture is to really try to have more empathy, and that means taking time to get to know people you disagree with.

MY EXPERIENCE IN THE CHURCH
Jeremy Erickson

Attraction to the same sex is something Christians must learn to deal with in community with others. Being open about one's sexuality is one of the best predictors of emotional health for sexual minorities. Yet the choice to be open is not enough—how people respond to that openness is also critical. In this piece, I'd like to focus on the responses from others, sharing what I have found helpful and where I have seen some responses harm.

I grew up in a fairly conservative Christian home. In my early teens, I started to figure out that I was attracted to people of both sexes. This was both confusing and difficult. While I had been taught to expect feelings for girls, feelings for other boys were out of the question. Steeped in conservative Christian culture, my parents had been taught that being gay was a choice that came from moral rebellion. I didn't feel safe talking about what I was going through at the time, and only later did I find helpful information from other same-sex-attracted Christians.

Fortunately, once I did start opening up, things went about as well as they could have. My parents were understanding, willing to learn and question their assumptions. As I've opened up more publicly and have had a growing ministry around sexuality, they've been a great support. This ministry is something we can and do talk about, but not something that has to dominate every conversation.

My experience with churches has also been mostly positive. I was not very open with my church community in college, but during graduate school I started to open up a lot more in my PCA (Presbyterian Church in America) church context. Two church leaders provided a lot of wisdom as I started opening up. We had several conversations about what ministry could look like for me. I had the opportunity to share my story in a Sunday school lesson, and later as part of a pastor's sermon. Similarly, at my current PCA church, the elders supported me in doing a Sunday school series on LGBTQ-related topics. And various Christians in my life have come to me with questions about their own LGBTQ friends and neighbors.

There are also some major pitfalls I haven't encountered nearly to the degree some of my friends have. For example, my churches have not compromised on biblical teaching regarding gay sex. However, people have generally been willing to listen and learn rather than digging their feet in. They haven't made mountains out of molehills when it comes to issues such as terminology. They've been willing to come alongside me through all the various joys and struggles of life rather than focusing on my sexuality as something I needed to "fix" before I could be fully included.

Not all of my friends have had the same positive experience. Several have been removed from positions of employment or leadership, even though they were living in line with an orthodox understanding of sexual ethics. Some have been socially excluded or ignored after talking about their sexuality. Some are taught that God expects them to repent of not just the way they handle their feelings but of their feelings themselves. When people don't escape to a church that can support them in holiness, they usually end up abandoning Christianity entirely. The church needs to understand that feelings for the same sex are often not the result of abusive situations or rebellious moral choices but are experienced involuntarily.

Where I think my church has done relatively well, though any American church needs to grow, is in providing more support and connection beyond just Sunday morning. Participating in small groups with a mix of married and single people has been a major blessing. Being included in various social get-togethers, providing hospitality myself, and knowing I have people I can call on if I need help have all been a huge blessing. But the lack of long-term stability can still be hard, even if getting married to a woman in the future is more of a possibility for me than for my gay or lesbian friends. My particular church congregations have done pretty well, but there is always room for improvement.

In general, I'm hopeful that churches and individual Christians can learn to do better. I've had a taste of what that can look like, and I exhort my fellow believers to consider how they can best love their sexual minority brothers and sisters.

Create a Healthy Culture for Single Christians

Although the concerns of celibate gay Christians are not always identical to the concerns of other unmarried Christians in the church, those who remain single because of their sexual identity and sexual ethics are a subset of a larger group of single Christians in the church. Part of making the church safe for celibate gay Christians, then, is making the church safe for all its unmarried members. Kyle Keating, a Side B blogger, discusses the need to establish a healthy culture for single persons in his blog post "What Makes a Church Safe?"

> In order for the church to be perceived as a viable alternative community to the ones . . . gays and lesbians are already in, she must make space for singles—and not just temporary singles, but people who feel called to a life of celibacy. Indeed, creating space for singles and thinking about the role of singleness in the church is a prerequisite to offering a viable and desirable apologetic to gay and lesbian people. If we are going to call them to give up relationships of deep intimacy, then we must be prepared to offer them a community of deep intimacy. Is our singles community simply a place where we try and solve the problem of singleness? Are we prepared to provide community for a forty-five-year-old single man or woman? A safe church thinks through these questions and considers how they might encourage deep friendships among congregants across all sorts of family lines. Everyone is longing for the deep connection of friendship (even married folks!) and friendship must play a key role in making a space for singles in the church.[2]

There are differences, of course, between being single and gay and being single and straight, but the culture for single Christians will impact the experiences of celibate gay Christians, and some of our interviewees commented on that. For example, Lucas related how a high view of singleness might be accompanied by a more accurate view of marriage:

> Whether the church has a healthy space for single Christians is an important question—trying to get away from sort of baptizing Hollywood romance and look more seriously at what the Bible says about marriage and celibacy. Also, I think [the church needs] a more realistic picture of marriage—so that it's not a romanticized picture of marriage. I think if there were more attention to both the positive elements and the challenges, then it would be easier to deal with the positives and challenges of celibacy.

Sebastian advised churches, "Be supportive of singles first and foremost. Be supportive of singles. If I could get to a church where a five-year-old could know that I was an adult and not married and did not think that was weird, I think I would have found a good church."

Charles reflected on the challenges that arise when the church defends marriage and denigrates singleness in the process:

> I think that the church has a problem, in that the church senses that the so-called "institution of marriage" is under attack, or certainly less valued in our culture, or people are less interested in marriage. They rush to try to defend marriage, and there is nothing wrong with that, but in so doing, they erase the other story [that honors singleness]. You know, by their general strategy of defending marriage, by saying it is the best thing and the awesomest thing ever, but you know the church has a lot of people besides just the homosexually attracted people who will never get married.

Identify and Affirm Spiritual Families

Part of honoring singleness within the church means recognizing that the nuclear biological family should not be the only—or even the primary—source of familial belonging in Christian communities. Interviewee Charles gave his thoughts on spiritual families:

When I read the Bible, what I constantly see is the Lord, or Jesus, affirming spiritual families of the church above the nuclear family. Like, he showed that your true home, your true family, your true brothers and sisters are the church and not your nuclear family. . . . I think that the American church, [in its efforts] to "focus on the family" or "protect the family," has really alienated a lot of people, and embitter[ed] people. . . . You're burdening them with unrealistic expectations, while not lifting a finger to help them carry the burden, as Jesus says to the Pharisees.

Ben advised the church "to focus less on the nuclear family and focus more broadly on what it means to be community with the broader church family, so that singles are not . . . only relegated to their kind of singles ministry or [left] to fend for themselves." Instead, Ben proposed, singles need to be organically incorporated into the lives of others in the church; he longed "to see a lot of married couples and married families see singles not as, *Oh, we should invite them over for dinner,* but like, *What if we went on vacation with them?*" Ben felt that there was a deep need "for same-sex-attracted people within the church to have those families [where they are welcomed as full participants] as opposed to being left to fend out there on their own."

Eugene shared the following suggestions for the church: "I hopefully will have really close friends, Christian brothers and sisters for sure. But someday I want to find my niche, who will be supportive of me, whether they're married or whatever, but hopefully having an established group of friends will mean I can just sit back, put my head on their shoulder, and just be comfortable. That's what I really want."

Maintain a Consistent Standard

Another piece of advice celibate gay Christians had for churches was that if they choose to confront same-sex sexual sin, they should be consistent in equally confronting other forms of sexual sin. Charles discussed the importance of consistency:

> The real danger is when people sense the church has a double standard. That in one sin area, the church is demanding obedience in cleaning up behaviors before they can participate in church life, whereas in other scenarios, the church is willing to overlook them. You know, the church that I went to in South Carolina, it did actually challenge people about homosexual practice of people in their leadership, but it only worked because everyone in the church knew that they also took heterosexual sex very seriously. They took greed very seriously. They took every sin issue equally as seriously. In fact, they were probably more willing to confront people about their heterosexual sin rather than their homosexual sin, just because of the social dynamic. And so that was, I think, really amazing, which wasn't the double standard, and people really need to believe that [same-sex sexual sin] is not any different from any other brokenness that humans experience.

Embrace a Latitude in Language

Our sample of celibate gay Christians also advised churches to invest less effort in policing the terminology of sexual minorities. Desmond stated,

One thing I would say; drop the language war. It wastes a lot of people's time and energy and, you know, whether to say "gay" or "same-sex attracted" or whatever. It wastes a lot of time and energy, it creates a lot of misunderstandings both for people who have to deal with it and their families, and between the Christians and LGBT people. And even if you win at the end, all you've got is that somebody says "same-sex attracted" instead of "gay." I do not think that's worth the headache. And it's not even that I care that much what people call themselves, it's that so many Christians make a big deal about what people call themselves that I think it discredits the church. And I think that this has a grain of truth in it, but it's not completely fair, but a lot of people think that because churches are so hostile to gay language, a lot of people assume that they're far more homophobic [than] they are. I don't think that the church is as homophobic as they come across. There's such a thing as having concerns about how people identify, but when it looks like you're uncomfortable with even using the word *gay*, that makes you look really bigoted. And I don't think the church needs that. Her teaching is hard enough without that. So that's a big thing. Another big thing, drop the hostility to coming out of the closet. I will give the Catholic Church some credit because she has never actually taught that it is wrong. You don't necessarily know that from talking to lots of Catholics.

Desmond raises many points that warrant elaboration. He is concerned about the time and energy put into monitoring language, which is one consideration, and he is also concerned about how such a focus affects those outside the church who already view Christians as homophobic.

Language is important and requires a bit of nuance. We want to connect Desmond's comments on language to Ron Belgau's discussion of the 1986 Letter to the Bishops of the Catholic Church on the Pastoral Care of Homosexual Persons.[3] The section Belgau interacts with reads:

> The human person, made in the image and likeness of God, can hardly be adequately described by a reductionist reference to his or her sexual orientation. Every one living on the face of the earth has personal problems and difficulties, but challenges to growth, strengths, talents and gifts as well. Today, the Church provides a badly needed context for the care of the human person when she refuses to consider the person as a "heterosexual" or a "homosexual" and insists that every person has a fundamental Identity: the creature of God, and by grace, his child and heir to eternal life. (§16)

In his review of this passage,[4] Belgau discusses the English translation and compares it to the original Latin and how it is translated in other languages. He offers a compelling argument that a better English translation would be that the Church refuses "to consider the person as *only* a 'heterosexual' or a 'homosexual.'" For Belgau, the implication is that, in keeping with the first part of the quote above, a person who experiences same-sex attraction cannot be reduced to their sexual orientation, which is apparently a concern raised by some Christian leaders when celibate gay Christians refer to themselves as "gay." At the same time, the person's sexual orientation "is a significant fact about the person." He goes on to write, "It's also notable that the phrase 'homosexual person' occurs 23 times in the document—most obviously in the title itself—and also in the *Catechism*. The Church obviously does not teach that you can't apply sexual orientation labels to persons. The key, however, is that the person is not *defined by* or *reducible to* their sexual orientation" (his emphasis).

We have found that many celibate gay Christians share the

concern that they not be reduced to their sexual attractions. At the same time, they do not experience the word *gay* as doing that, at least not in the way that many Christians may be concerned about. We have found at least six distinct reasons why celibate gay Christians have preferred to use the word *gay*, though we would caution that this is not an exhaustive list. The first reason they use the label is for clarity and simplicity: *gay* has become the common vernacular for describing one's sexual orientation. Celibate gay Christians, then, see themselves as simply using language as it is being used today by the majority of English speakers.

A second reason for using the label is a dislike of the descriptive phrase ("I experience same-sex attraction") as reductionistic. They believe that the word *gay* accurately captures additional aspects of their experience, interests, and personality that cannot be reduced to who they are attracted to sexually. In other words, "same-sex attraction" is too narrow and simplistic.

Another reason they prefer the word *gay* is because descriptive language (e.g., "I'm same-sex attracted" or "I experience SSA") has at times been associated with an ex-gay narrative, and insofar as celibate gay Christians do not mean to communicate that as a frame of reference, they prefer a different term that better describes how they think of themselves and also how they relate to others, including those in the broader LGBTQ+ community.

A fourth reason is that celibate gay Christians do indeed share some commonalities with other gay persons and with certain aspects of the LGBTQ+ community, and the word *gay* captures some of that nuance. As we have already noted, there are clear differences between gay celibate Christians and the mainstream LGBTQ+ community, but there are also some shared understandings and experiences.

A fifth reason is more missional in nature. Some individuals use the term to be a more visible presence for other, younger Christians who are gay and do not know that there are people out there who can be a testimony to God's presence and faithfulness in their lives apart from testimonies of change or healing. Along with this, some prefer to describe themselves as gay because they view the LGBTQ+ community as a mission field of sorts, and they prefer to use language that gives them access to others for whom their testimony might have an effect.

We understand that the language LGBTQ+ individuals use to describe their experiences will continue to be an ongoing topic of discussion in the church today. What we sense from conversations with some of our interviewees is a need for more latitude in the use of language, while finding better and more nuanced ways to engage how language functions in the lives of celibate gay Christians.

Focus on Intentional, Individual Ministry

Some of our interviewees also proposed that churches abandon attempts to change Western culture and instead focus their efforts on ministry to individual people. Desmond advised,

Concentrate on reaching individual people rather than society at large. Because I think one of the things that has created the insanely destructive culture war is this idea, which I consider to be a quite false idea, that if we Christianize the culture, then the people will come with it. And the common corollary to that, that the way to Christianize the culture is by doing it through politics. I don't think that's true. I think that the only way to reach culture is to reach individual people who then reach other individual people. And I think that eventually, if Christians are loving Christ—and, by association, loving their neighbor—that will Christianize a society by degrees, by people. And I think that if a society is Christianized for a long enough period, it will eventually be reflected in politics. It is my own opinion based on history and philosophy, my view of reality, that it has to work in that direction and that it cannot work the other way. And I think that Christians have been trying to make it work the other way for most of history in this country. And I'm deeply convinced that that doesn't work at all. It doesn't mean that you don't fight political injustice, but that's not the same thing as trying to baptize the political system.

Jean agreed on the importance of reaching out to individual people, offering a vision of what such outreach might entail: "I'd like to see [outreach] be more intentional, and maybe inviting somebody else in more long-term to live here . . . or simply [see] who needs a place, and we can meet a need in a time when somebody needs it. A practical thing. Having our home be a place that people can retreat to, that people can show up unexpectedly at, you know."

Identify and Minister to What We Have in Common

Some of our interviewees expressed that some of their churches supported them well by focusing on the commonalities between gay and straight sexual sin. That is, those who struggle with same-sex sexual sin and those who struggle with other kinds of sexual sin, including run-of-the-mill heterosexual sin. Jean discussed the common ground she felt with other church members in such an environment: "I've found a lot of freedom to almost compare notes or to have something to offer that friend, that girlfriend of mine who has been married fifteen years and has four kids, and suddenly we can—we can talk about our sexual brokenness as something in common, not as something that I have."

This shift in attitude, Jean proposed, gives same-sex-oriented people like herself a wider realm of resources and experiences from which to draw: "So that helps to kind of look at other examples of brokenness or examples of how the world is now, subsequent to the fall, in that your unique experience is not one that would isolate you or that is so out of the norm that it has to have this other way of looking at things, but you can kind of compare it to other people's experiences and make sense of it that way."

Adopt an Intentional, Missional Focus

Several of those we interviewed emphasized the value of building intentional relationships with LGBTQ+ people. Jean framed the idea this way:

> If you have neighbors across the street that you know they're a lesbian couple that got married this summer. I don't know, I don't think there's anything wrong with moving toward them because of that fact. And not the neighbors next to you that . . . for whatever reason are a lot more like you. Because it's unnatural, I guess. It would be more natural to move toward the next-door neighbors, you know—they kind of look like you when you look in the mirror and not across the street. But for that very reason, I would say—I don't know. Take the pumpkin bread to the people across the street.

Jean added later in her interview,

> So in the same way, when we show up with our Bible verses and know-how and try to—you know, with the intent of being the rescuers—you know, we're going to rescue, we're going to convert, we're going to bring them to church, welcome them in the faith. I just think, well, by God's grace, maybe that happens sometimes, but I think, let's just call it what it is and say, "Hey, I don't know much about what you're doing over here. Like, I want to move closer and not, hopefully, not in a selfish way, but . . . so I can understand it better. Not because I'm going to swoop in and fix you, but because I need to learn more." And maybe there's room for us to learn from each other.

Alex agreed that Christians need to purposefully reach out to LGBTQ+ people beyond their church community. "I think the church is afraid of interacting with the wider queer community," he said. He urged Christians to "be willing to make dialogue with people . . . be willing to reach out . . . [say,] 'We apologize if the church has hurt you but God loves [you]' . . . really simple things like that where you're willing to put yourself out there and have the humility to hear their perspectives."

Eugene had the following suggestions for the church:

> We should always, in terms of society, we should be saying, "Come here and really be a community, and let's share in Christ's love, and we're all broken, we are all broken, we all struggle with different sins," so church should be humble in that way, I think. Church should be humble in accepting people. Even if they aren't on Side B, they should talk about knowing Christ more, and I know it's kind of contradictory to what I was saying before about the whole conversation of homosexuality, [but] I think the conversation has to be open enough where the pastor of the church can accept them without passing judgment on the couple at the church door.

ON BEING INTENTIONAL

We have looked in this chapter at what pastors say is needed in their churches, followed by several recommendations from celibate gay Christians. We should point out that we have much less information from pastors than we do from celibate gay Christians about what they believe is needed. Also, some of the requests and recommendations made by these two groups appear to be on different tracks altogether, which is a concern. Some pastors frame same-sex sexual identity as a sin and hope to refer their sexual minority congregants to outside experts for counseling. Many of the same pastors also seek answers about the causes of same-sex sexuality. But it is worth noting that none of these approaches matches the experiences and recommendations of celibate gay Christians, though much of their theology aligns with that of the pastors in their churches.

As we consider how these differences in approach and perspective might be handled in the church, we want to look at some of the recommendations researchers have made. One of the most relevant recommendations we see in existing research is that of *intentionality*.

For more than ten years, we at the Institute for the Study of Sexual Identity have listened to the experiences of students who navigate sexual identity and faith on Christian college campuses.[5] What we have concluded from our research is that Christian institutions could consider how to be more *intentional*: intentionally *relational*, intentionally *formational*, and intentionally *secure*. What do these principles mean, and how can we apply them to the challenge facing the church today?

The experiences of Christians navigating faith and sexual identity in Christian institutions is *interpersonally mediated*. This means that the quality of the relationships people have directly impacts the quality of their experience in a Christian institution. Because of this, we advised Christian institutions to be intentionally relational, prioritizing their students' relational needs in order to improve the quality of students' experiences. Taking this insight from a Christian college or university campus and applying it to the local church, we would encourage churches to be more relational as well, a theme we will pick up in chapter 6. Ironically, it may be that the relational gifts of celibate gay Christians are precisely what are needed to make the church more relational. This is an idea we will return to in chapter 7.

To be intentionally formational, we proposed in our previous research to focus on Christian discipleship and, more broadly, to take a "whole person" approach to sexual minorities on Christian college campuses. For the church, this might mean becoming a place where people truly grow in depth and in the sincerity of their faith. In Catholic churches, this means inviting sexual minorities into a sacramental approach to spiritual formation. In Protestant churches, where much of spiritual formation is in the study of Scripture (individually and in small group Bible studies), corporate worship, and prayer, sexual minorities could likewise be invited into these formational spaces as whole people in need of discipleship in the same way every other church member is invited. The more time the church members spend together, the more opportunity they have to build closer relationships. We have found time and time again that celibate gay Christians, by virtue of the costly obedience they live out every day, bring to the body of Christ a sincerity and maturity to their walk with Christ that could strengthen the larger church.

When we suggested being "intentionally secure" in our research on college students, we were talking about providing physical, emotional, and spiritual security for everyone in the campus community.[6] We cannot grow in a healthy manner when we don't feel safe. From an attachment-based perspective, a person's security is fostered when they have a community that provides a safe haven (or a reliable relational milieu) or a secure base (reliable relational foundations).[7] Likewise, a spiritual environment is healthy when it reduces our anxieties and fear-based ways of being present with one another. If churches want to be intentional in providing these environments, we need greater security in our faith communities, in our small groups, in the administration of our churches, and in what we relate in our teaching. Lecture-based theological presentations may not accurately model the emotional and relational commitment that is needed to engage in productive discussions about sexual identity and faith. Such presentations can risk coming across as "authoritarian" rather than as authoritative teachings of Christian doctrine.[8] Emotional, relational engagement with gay individuals may be more difficult or costly to the supportive friend or pastor, but willingness to stand in an uncomfortable place of tension may exhibit more love and compassion than the alternative of further theological discussion. Those who teach on these subjects in the church need to assume there are people in the room (and in the broader congregation) who are actively navigating questions of sexual identity and faith, and they must seek to intentionally humanize the discussion while teaching Christian doctrine.

This kind of intentional culture—relational, formational, and secure—is a step toward fostering a church climate where individuals and the greater church communities are equipped to develop and mature as they engage questions at the intersection of faith and sexuality. Theologically, this can be thought of as an intentionally Trinitarian community.[9] People need places in the church where they experience institutional support. Doctrinal positions can create community-wide behavioral boundaries that articulate the church's historical teaching on sexual ethics and provide support for the person living out that teaching. Yet even with well-articulated doctrines, the person navigating sexual-identity questions will also need secure structures and relational spaces in the faith community if they are to remain true to their commitments without compromising their emotional or spiritual health. It is especially important for pastors, priests, deacons, elders, and other church leaders to be approachable and supportive and to model for their communities how sexual minorities ought to be received.

Intentional church climates that provide security for celibate gay Christians must also reflect relational cultural competence.[10] Rather than patently denouncing the LGBTQ+ community, church leaders who want to welcome celibate gay Christians should reflect a more nuanced approach, offering doctrinal clarity about sexuality and sexual behavior while also fostering relationships that are respectful of LGBTQ+ persons who disagree with those doctrines. Churches with a historically traditional outlook on sexuality may be tempted to focus on policing language. Rather than emotionally reacting to the broader culture wars and the affront of sexual permissiveness, pastors who practice relational cultural competence find ways to love people even within a changing cultural landscape.

Celibate gay Christians want to know that their faith community understands and appreciates them as people and is there to help them navigate their faith journey. Pastors must communicate that they value celibate gay Christians as people of faith whose same-sex sexuality is real and challenging. Many of these individuals are striving to live faithfully before God, and like other believers they experience God's presence, provision, and grace and are growing in spiritual maturity. They are ready to share their spiritual gifts to help strengthen the body of Christ. They have an experience of God's grace that is valuable and needed in the church, and any blueprint that excludes this possibility will exclude the vast majority of celibate gay Christians from embracing their place in the church.

CONCLUSION

In the first part of this chapter, we considered how pastors frame the topic of sexual identity and what pastors say they focus on and what they think is needed for ministry to people navigating same-sex sexuality. We then listened to advice from celibate gay Christians. We noted that these two groups may be speaking past one another on a few key points, particularly if pastors focus more on causation, frame sexuality primarily in terms of sin, or plan to refer gay Christians to specialists. While the theology of both groups may align in many respects (in terms of what sexual behaviors are morally permissible and morally impermissible), there is still much that is not being approached in a like-minded manner. We close the chapter by considering how the church could be more intentional toward people who identify as celibate gay Christians. We propose that churches that are intentionally relational, formational, and secure in their welcoming of people who are navigating same-sex sexuality will be best situated to move forward in love as pastors and celibate gay Christians address their differences in perspective and approach.

FOR DISCUSSION

1. What are the obstacles to developing a single blueprint that all churches could follow that would address the concerns of celibate gay Christians?

2. Consider what pastors said in this chapter. What else do you think pastors look for when it comes to same-sex sexuality and the church? Is what they are looking for a good match for what celibate gay Christians recommend? Why or why not?

3. Of the recommendations from celibate gay Christians for the church, which recommendation stood out to you as most important and why? Are the recommendations from celibate gay Christians a good match for what pastors are asking for? Why or why not?

4. How are the three aspects of intentionality (relational, formational, and secure) related to each other?

CHAPTER 6

CELIBATE GAY CHRISTIANS
and REAL LIFE

What I feared most, though, about my decision to remain celibate was that I had thereby doomed myself to lifelong loneliness. When I was still in high school, despite being gay, I often daydreamed about what it would be like to be married, to have a house and children, to have a home of the sort I had growing up, to know that I belonged somewhere. Now, in light of where I felt my Christian faith was taking me, I stopped dreaming about those things. In their place, I began to have a recurrent picture of myself around age sixty, coming home to an empty apartment, having lived all of my adulthood as a single man. I started to think about the particulars of that scenario: not knowing each year where I'd be for Christmas, waking up each morning to a quiet bedroom and having no one across the table from me as I ate my cereal before heading to work, coming home at the end of the day and reading a book with no one to talk to about the parts of it that stood out to me. I began to resonate with what Lauren Winner has called "the loneliness of the everyday": "the loneliness of no one knowing if your plane lands on time, of no one to call if you lock yourself out of your house or your alternator dies—I find that loneliness worse [than the loneliness that comes as a result of a breakup or a divorce]."

And I began to wonder what, if anything, to do about it.

Wesley Hill[1]

In this chapter, we will explore how sexual majority Christians respond to the lived reality of celibate gay Christians. We first want to consider this question at the personal level: How do individuals interact with and respond to one another? We will discuss institutional considerations in the next chapter.

Let's summarize some of what we have learned to this point. We have seen that celibate gay Christians are living a costly form of obedience by following (however imperfectly) a traditional Christian sexual ethic that restricts sex to marriage between male and female. As with anyone embracing a life of repentance and seeking to conform to the ethical standard of Christ, they share many commonalities with all believers who share this sexual ethic, especially single heterosexuals. As individuals we face varied temptations and struggles, but those navigating same-sex sexuality and faith face unique challenges. More specifically, as we have seen in our research sample, they face challenges with attachment and the importance of interpersonal relationships. With regard to the question of attachment, we found great diversity among celibate gay Christians. We found that a preoccupied attachment style was the most common attachment style among celibate gay Christians, followed by the secure and fearful-avoidant styles.

Preoccupied attachment style. Persons having a preoccupied attachment style want intimacy, want to be in relationships with others, but they also worry about those relationships. This is certainly understandable when we consider the likelihood that many have experienced rejection. These individuals can grow in their awareness of their relational insecurities, and close, enduring friendships will, by definition, provide stability that will assuage worries.

Secure attachment style. When people have a secure attachment style, they tend to seek out relationships and are not especially anxious about those relationships. They are better positioned emotionally to regulate their affect. They tend to be comfortable with others and also when they are by themselves.

Fearful-avoidant attachment style. Those who are fearful-avoidant in their attachment style are not typically as comfortable with close, intimate relationships, and they are less likely to pursue such relationships. In close friendships, they may need to be given more space from time to time. As with those who have a preoccupied attachment style, they may have a lower view of themselves that can at times complicate interpersonal relationships.

In addition to noting the unique challenges of each attachment style, we believe that a sustained relationship is an essential starting point for developing healthy interactions with gay celibate individuals. Friendships cannot be treated lightly or with indifference; they must be a source of investment that is sustained over time. If insecurities are present, people who form close friendships can recognize and understand insecurities without holding insecurity against their friends. In addition to committing to a sustained relationship and understanding possible insecurities, being a source of encouragement is also important. This seems obvious, but many gay Christians have experienced rejection and continue to encounter silence or negative exchanges in their faith communities. Is it possible that an insecure attachment pattern is almost unavoidable for many celibate gay Christians who find themselves in shaming and precarious family/church cultures? Put differently, is what we refer to as an insecure attachment pattern essentially a "survival response" to family/church conditions that do not allow for the alleviation of fear? To relate to others through more secure attachment patterns may be somewhat of a mystery to followers of Christ who are navigating same-sex sexuality in a traditional faith setting. There may be ways we do things in the church that contribute to insecure interactional trajectories.[2]

Keep in mind that many celibate gay Christians wonder what

people think when they disclose this part of their lives to them. For many of them, by virtue of firsthand experience, even what has been experienced as a good friendship is up for grabs once disclosure of same-sex sexuality takes place. So while we can offer a few thoughts on responding to different attachment styles, before we elaborate further on fostering healthy relationships, let's first take a look at how some celibate gay Christians view the support they currently receive.

We asked celibate gay Christians about their satisfaction with the level of support they receive (1) in general and (2) with respect to their same-sex sexuality. We asked them about support from family, their church, straight friends, and other gay friends. On a six-point Likert scale, our sample could select the degree to which they agreed or disagreed with a statement about their current level of satisfaction with the support they receive, both in general and with respect to their same-sex sexuality. We then collapsed their agreement (ranging from strongly to slightly agree) or disagreement (ranging from strongly to slightly disagree) into "agree" or "disagree."

We can see in table 6.1 that about two-thirds or more of our sample of celibate gay Christians agree that they are currently satisfied with the general level of social support they receive. This is not specific to same-sex sexuality; rather, it is just general support covering any number of areas of life. A higher percentage of our sample reported agreement in terms of general support from straight friends in their lives. We did not see differences by type of celibacy.

We can see in table 6.2, however, that the percentages change when asking about support for same-sex attractions. For some sources of support, the percentages reflecting agreement/disagreement almost flip. We can see that nearly two-thirds disagree that they are satisfied with the support they receive for their same-sex attractions from their families or from the church.

TABLE 6.1. AGREEMENT/DISAGREEMENT THAT CELIBATE GAY CHRISTIAN IS CURRENTLY SATISFIED WITH GENERAL LEVEL OF SOCIAL SUPPORT

Source of Support	Agree		Disagree	
	n	Percent	n	Percent
Family	200	67.6	96	32.4
Church	199	67.5	96	32.5
Straight friends	242	82.0	53	18.0
Gay friends	185	65.4	98	34.6

A higher percentage agree they are satisfied with support from friends, especially straight friends. The difference in agreement for straight and gay friends is interesting. While we do not know the reason for this difference, we can speculate that it may reflect the complicated relationship celibate gay Christians have with the LGBTQ+ community.

We ran some additional analyses on the relationship between support and depression and anxiety, and we found that there does appear to be a correlation. Participants who were moderately or severely depressed had less support from family, church, and friends than those who were not depressed or only mildly depressed.

TABLE 6.2. AGREEMENT/DISAGREEMENT THAT CELIBATE GAY CHRISTIAN IS CURRENTLY SATISFIED WITH LEVEL OF SOCIAL SUPPORT REGARDING SAME-SEX SEXUALITY

Source of Support	Agree		Disagree	
	n	Percent	n	Percent
Family	106	37.1	180	62.9
Church	104	36.1	184	63.9
Straight friends	194	66.9	96	33.1
Gay friends	161	57.5	119	42.5

We saw similar trends among those who were anxious, although we had a smaller number of anxious participants that precluded us from running analyses.

Let's get at some of the underlying issues in these results by asking a question. If people are expected to live out a biblical sexual ethic, how will that choice be supported by people who are close to them? To begin exploring this, we interviewed several friends who function as family to celibate gay Christians. Their perspectives add an important dimension to the discussion in the church about what it means to live out the costly obedience of faithfulness to Christ as a gay and celibate individual. In a society where friendships tend to be rather thin or are reduced to "likes" on social media, these individuals offer a remarkable and indispensable gift to celibate gay Christians. As we have come to learn, friendships are especially important in the lives of those who are single, and celibate gay Christians who anticipate a life of singleness are in search of healthy and sustainable ways to experience intimacy within singleness. To understand how celibate gay Christians can be supported, we would like to better understand the formation of friendships that function as family relationships in the lives of celibate gay Christians.

WHEN FRIENDS TRANSFORM INTO FAMILY

When we interviewed several friends who function as family to celibate gay Christians, we were able to identify themes that contributed to the increasing depth and significance of their friendship over time. We might think of these themes as characteristics of the formation of family relationships among friends. In connecting this to our earlier discussion of attachment, we are laying a trajectory for churches that want to help people move from insecure to secure attachment. Recognizing that the friendships we observed took many different forms is important. Some were friendships between a married couple and a celibate gay Christian. Others involved a single close friend and a celibate gay Christian. Still others involved some form of communal life together. There is no single way of being a Christian family together, although different forms are likely to meet different needs, according to the unique circumstances of the people involved.

In any case, when we interviewed friends who function as family in the lives of celibate gay Christians, we saw the following characteristics. These characteristics are not stages that every friendship goes through; rather, these are some of the key experiences, or milestones, that friends often (but not always) identified as important when they looked back on the life of their friendship. The characteristics include: (1) extending invitations, (2) developing friendship, (3) living (or inviting to live) in proximity, (4) increasing tension, and (5) increasing intimacy.

Extending Invitations

This first milestone, extending invitations, may seem obvious, but friendships do not just happen. In fact, many relationships we think of as friendships are likely better described as acquaintances, which is perhaps an indictment of the shallowness of our friendships today. To move from being acquainted with someone to being a friend requires several points of contact in everyday life. These points of contact may occur in school, at church activities, in places of employment, or elsewhere. Some forms of structured contact, such as being in college together, are harder to come by as people grow older. The closeness of the relationship typically depends on the amount of time spent together: the more time spent together, the closer the relationship.

While points of contact are essential to the evolution of a friendship, they are insufficient in themselves to create a friendship. People who become friends must at some point spend intentional time together, which means that someone must extend an invitation to be together. This is where we found the first milestone in the development of familial friendships with celibate gay Christians—the extension of an invitation to spend time together. These invitations need not be formal; they are simply the natural, common invitations that people offer one another, the kinds of invitations that, if accepted, can create opportunities to discover relational chemistry or points of common interest.

Not everyone in the church will extend such an invitation to a celibate gay Christian individual. Indeed, the initiative taken to extend the invitation says a lot about the person or couple or family extending it.[3] One couple we interviewed told us that they have been family to a celibate gay Christian and told us that they "have a long history of trying to practice hospitality." Hospitable practices are often imbued with spiritual significance. The husband in another couple we interviewed said, "What we were doing at home—it was based off of our spiritual life. . . . We made a point to bring people in hospitality, a lot of reaching out."

Developing Friendship

The second milestone we observed had to do with the development of the friendship. Those who became family to celibate gay Christians indicated that they did not experience the friendship as a discrete addition to an otherwise unchanged life. Instead, the friendship became impactful enough that it changed everyone involved. One couple we interviewed said, "This friendship is unique in that there is a high likelihood . . . we will continue to change what we would have done in life because of this friendship." Another interviewee, William, spoke of his family's relationship with a male celibate gay Christian: "So that's been a very formative relationship to this day now, and he's been very much a part of our family and family dynamics. He doesn't live with us, but our family has been that for him." Still another friend we interviewed,

James, offered, "I think too that it has taught me to be a better friend and what it means to listen and to care and to be committed to someone even when they don't want to share, even when they're afraid, even when relationships are risky."

Living (or Inviting to Live) in Proximity

Friends who function as family do not necessarily have to live together, although we found that shared living arrangements were the norm for some of the people we interviewed. Yet even among friends who lived under separate roofs there was a sense that being close to one another mattered in these friendships. Physical proximity is a hallmark of family life, and some of the friendships we observed benefited from doing life together.

Several interviewees mentioned how living near each other was significant to their friendship. One couple, Jeffrey and Angie, developed a relationship with a celibate gay Christian man who intentionally moved to a new residence so he could live in closer proximity to them. Jeffrey said, "He decided it would be healthier to move closer to us." Angie and Jeffrey felt that proximity was especially important to this friendship. Jeffrey clarified, "[This celibate gay Christian] would be the only person of all of my friends that we are contemplating the possibility of what it might look like to actually stay together over years and decades and be in the same place, whether that's in the same house or the close vicinity."

In some of the friendships we learned about, living in proximity led to an invitation to live together. Jeffrey and Angie told the story of how they had half-jokingly suggested that they could move in with their gay friend. Their gay friend responded that he would love that; shortly after that conversation, they were moving their things in to live together. Jeffrey and Angie had lived with housemates for much of their married life, Angie explained, "so it wasn't a stretch to think in terms of doing life together in this way."

Wyatt, who, together with his wife, opened his home for a

celibate gay woman, shared the circumstances behind that move: "When she was in college, my wife and I asked her and her sister to move in with us due to a difficult family situation that they had."

Sometimes living together also meant buying a house together. Although this wasn't a common experience among our interviewees, Jackson told us that the "last milestone [in my friendship with a celibate gay Christian] was buying this house together. In some ways, there is a milestone every six months. . . . It's all new territory for both of us."

Increasing Tension

Another milestone noted by friends, and one that is a natural aspect of any deep and developing friendship, is the inevitable emergence of tensions and points of conflict. Jackson said,

> The next milestone would be a really heated discussion we had because she just didn't trust me about anything, and I was trying to figure out why. . . . "Why then have you moved in with us?" She explained, "I want to be in relationship with you. I don't know how to make this work." And that was probably the biggest milestone. Talking through . . . unforgiveness over my hurting her, and that until she learned to forgive me and trust me just a little bit, [there was] not much we could do.

Another friend, Michael, discussed how he and his celibate gay friend came to a better understanding of their different ways of processing information: "I had to learn after a while, he wasn't being mean, he was just processing things differently. . . . It was me learning how to understand him." Still another friend, Carter, shared, "We had some issues with clinginess and me needing some space, and it was uncomfortable a little bit, and we had some difficult conversations, but we got a lot closer because of it."

Increasing Intimacy

Living in close proximity and working through the resulting tensions brought many friends to a place of greater intimacy. One friend, Evelyn, commented,

> I feel like we've developed a relationship of honesty and feedback so when either of us are struggling with something, we know we can reach out to the other person and talk through it and be honest about it. And there are really, I think from both sides, a lack of—there's not judgmentalism going on. So it's like, you know, being the type of people [who are] okay with where you're at [in] the times of struggle or hard times, so I think there's [an] open and supportive stance in that way.

Ian, another friend, said,

> I would say we both have matured over the years, which, that's a good thing. And I think that coming with that maturity is an ability to see greater nuance in these types of topics surrounding the LGBT—not that our conversations are only on that, obviously—but there's been more nuance and a greater appreciation on both of our parts and a greater complexity on the range of things involved in the LGBT discussions. And by that, I mean orientation, identity, dating, marriage—I mean, there's just a vast amount of topics that are bundled underneath this area.

Hannah, a woman we interviewed who was in a covenant relationship with a celibate gay Christian, reported, "For me, being in a relationship like that has also taught me to share God's love with others, especially to nonbelievers as well. I'd say the past six months has been a pretty dominant experience for me to learn how to love others sacrificially beyond the primary relationships that I am a part of."

On Taking a Vow of Celibacy
William Summay

When I first began trying to understand what it meant to embrace the vocation of celibacy and attempt to live it out, I knew I risked being misunderstood. Celibacy is a visible and countercultural way of life, and for some people in the gay community, it is seen as a way for the church to keep a tight leash on gay Christians or it is used by gay Christians themselves to justify their existence within the church. I knew that by seeking to live celibate I was going against the grain. My hope was to reclaim the rich and complex meaning of this ancient vocation. My studies eventually guided me to a decision to take formal, ceremonial vows within my church.

Before I became a vowed celibate, I knew my path forward would be unique. I knew that most people would see my being gay as the primary reason for my choice, and that proved to be true. Several people told me that they would never consider vows of celibacy because they did not struggle with their sexual identity. Others felt that I was clinging to a "biblical conservatism" by taking these vows. These responses confirmed for me that today in the Protestant church the decision to be celibate is viewed as a "gay thing," that its purpose is to publicly declare, "I am gay, but I am not having sex." Celibacy functions as a criterion of membership for gay people in the Protestant church today.

For me, however, the decision to take vows of celibacy meant embodying opposition to a variety of ways of being in the church, confronting ways of thinking that have largely been unquestioned, such as the idolization of marriage, the spiritualization of a mechanistic sexual ethic, and the place and treatment of the "other" in the Christian community. Celibacy, as I have come to understand it, cannot be grounded in impersonal and uncritical theologies but forces upon the church a reorientation toward a more communal way of operating, one that provides the means for the flourishing of the celibate person and their community. The good news is that this is a mutually sanctifying experience. This flourishing is dependent upon my personhood embodying the vowed-celibate vocation *and* the response of the community in which I find myself, since my vows include the commitment of my church community as well, covenanting to uphold me in keeping my vows.

Two realities have emerged since my decision to remain celibate. First, I've felt less pressure to prove myself to straight people and instead have been geared toward our mutual flourishing and what that means as someone who is a vowed celibate. Secondly, my decision has required fresh thinking in my church community. They've had to learn how to step into my celibate world and to think about how best to engage and support the flourishing of those who embrace the celibate life. Celibacy is not simply about the vowed celibate. It is an opportunity for the entire community to learn how to live a new life, one that confronts the embedded systems within the church. This paradigm shift has helped us to reorient celibacy away from being a "gay thing" and toward a "Christian thing," examining the ways in which celibacy makes demands on all of us to sacrifice comfort and certainty for the sake of holiness and obedience to Christ.

SUGGESTIONS

To assess how friendships can meet some of the emotional needs of celibate gay Christians, we also wanted to hear the insights of friends who are doing this well. What goes into a healthy, successful friendship? Feedback we received from several friends of celibate gay Christians suggested that *level of commitment, listening/ being receptive, being family,* and *being a good friend* were all components of building stronger bonds.

Level of Commitment

The first insight offered by our interviewees was to understand that the *level of commitment* involved in these relationships exceeds that of most friendships. Jeffrey, the husband in one couple we interviewed, said, "We love each other, we think of each other in terms of family. . . . The kind of sacrifice that one of us might have to make to make this work out over the long term is something we are thinking through and coming to grips with." Another friend, Michael, suggested that an intimate friendship with a celibate gay Christian requires taking the long view into consideration: "It's similar to any long-term relationship. . . . This is a long-term prospect. You're committing to someone long term. . . . We're not used to committing to people. . . . We're not used to being in relationships, intimate relationships with people who are not our spouse."

Jackson, a friend who eventually bought a house together with a celibate gay Christian, offered a similar suggestion:

Plan to be in it for the long term. . . . [Plan] to be honest about issues [that] come up but to be committed to working through things in good ways and being verbal about that. When [my celibate gay Christian friend] first moved back from college, what does this look like for us to live together?

It was good for us to process. It was good for her to hear us process: "We love living with you and enjoy you. . . . We enjoy you, and for as long as this works for us . . . we would love to do life together."

Listening/Being Receptive

A second suggestion these friends offered was to listen without trying to change the other person. One friend said, "Be ready to listen. . . . Drop notions of correction. . . . Just be able to listen and to engage them as a person and . . . be ready for nuance. . . . Things aren't necessarily so black and white like they often are in so many other aspects of our lives." Another friend offered the following: "My experience with more than one gay follower of Christ is that their ability to disclose many other things depends on the receptivity of their disclosure of this piece of their identity."

Still another friend offered a similar suggestion: "Be in a listening posture with people and not in a 'I want to try to help you' [or] 'I want you healed from this' [or] 'I want to point out that you could get married to someone' [posture] that we tend to want to do with people. [Learn] to listen well and not talk until you are invited to."

Being Family

A third suggestion we heard in our interviews was to try to offer to your friend the kinds of support and interaction that happen naturally in a family, or even in a marriage. One friend, Wyatt, explained:

Much of life is built around marriage. Celibate gay Christians—
or anyone who is single, by choice or not—need additional
support and relationships. It has been great for us to have [a
celibate gay Christian friend] as part of our family for someone to come home to, people to be excited about life events,

someone to take you to the hospital or care for you when you are sick, or just the multitude of things that married couples take for granted."

Wyatt said later in the interview, "The key for us is that we have made a family together."

Although the idea of family was important in these relationships, our interviewees cautioned against overidentifying with specific family roles, such as being a parent to another adult. Jackson said,

> I had a discussion with our associate pastor where he would say, "In effect you guys are Christian parents. [You] fill a lot of roles." Neither of us feel parental toward [our celibate gay Christian friend]. Because of the ways we have shared life . . . we feel very much like peers. . . . She hates any sort of parental-ness from us.

This is an important caution. Avoid condescending or disrespectful comments as well as assumptions about the nature of the relationship. Celibate gay Christians ought to be respected as adults and valued as peers. Indeed, as we will develop in chapter 7, celibate gay Christians offer unique gifts to the body of Christ, and this fact should challenge a posture of condescension or an overprotectiveness some might feel toward them.

Being a Good Friend

The fourth suggestion our interviewees made was just to be a good friend, especially when sexual-identity issues threaten to complicate the relationship. This means not being fearful or judgmental about the celibate gay Christian's experience of sexuality and not becoming overly concerned with putting labels on the friend. One friend, James, said,

There's not a need to be afraid. They, I mean, they're Christians, so they're brothers and sisters, and they're loved by God, and they're people with community, and they're not, like, crazy different. . . . I think [supportive friendships are] necessary not only for people who are gay but [also] for people who aren't gay, because I think there can be a sense of loneliness or isolation and anyone who would . . . identify as Christian, you need people in your life supporting you in unique ways.

Michael suggested not getting caught up in labels: "I think part of it would be not to fear them or overlabel them or define them. People who describe themselves as celibate gay Christians— sometimes we lock ourselves in with labels. . . . Look at your friend as your friend."

James offered the following:

Everyone has their unique struggles and their unique challenges. . . . They need people to come alongside of them and carry that with them . . . to be a source of comfort, to be a source of empathy, and there's no exception for people who identify as gay or celibate. While non-gay people may not be able to name what that experience is like, I think they play a vital role in allowing gay celibate Christians to participate in the body of Christ and to know that they're loved and [to experience] the love of God and the fellowship of saints. I think it is vital and necessary to make a point to become part of the [lives of] people who are celibate gay Christians.

The characteristics of the kinds of family relationships that can form from friendships are an important consideration for anyone who wishes to help people on a journey from insecure to secure attachment. These can be thought of as "healing" engagements that foster a more secure attachment over time. It should be noted that there is a dynamic here in which we see a combination of person and situation in healing, so this is also going to be important as we look at the church in the next chapter. A friend who functions as family is both available and responsive in keeping with the attachment literature. In this literature there is significant data showing that people benefit from having others who are close, available, and responsive, which helps not only in that moment but over time in areas such as self-esteem, interactions with others, and personal growth.[4]

CONCLUSION

In this chapter, we drew upon our findings on attachment styles and well-being among celibate gay Christians to consider how these factors might inform the interpersonal relationships of celibate gay Christians. We looked at what celibate gay Christians thought about the social support they receive in general and specifically regarding their same-sex sexuality from family, the church, straight friends, and gay friends. We then shared information from friends who function as family to celibate gay Christians and considered how those friendships developed intimacy over time. We listened to friends sharing suggestions and recommendations for friends who wish to function as family to celibate gay Christians. Our findings offer hope that although life-giving relationships may not come automatically to celibate gay Christians, such relationships can indeed be intentionally pursued and fostered over time.

FOR DISCUSSION

1. How might the current cultural climate (in society and in the church) concerning sexual identity and faith exacerbate attachment dynamics present among many celibate gay Christians?

2. How does an understanding of common attachment styles provide insight into what it may mean to be in close relationship with celibate gay Christians?

3. What makes level of commitment such an important point of discussion when being a friend who functions as family to a celibate gay Christian?

4. One challenge that exists has to do with establishing adult-to-adult relationships with celibate gay Christians rather than functioning as de facto parent figures or mimicking other family roles in some way. What are some strategies you could employ to retain a peer relationship?

CHAPTER 7

HOW CELIBATE GAY CHRISTIANS COULD STRENGTHEN *the* CHURCH

Maybe the problem isn't that gay Christians have received an impossible task [in their calling to lifelong celibacy]. Maybe the problem is that so many straight Christians have given themselves a task that is too easy, a cross that's too bearable. While gay Christians are expected to deny themselves in their desires for sex and family and intimacy—desires that feel so intrinsically part of their being—most straight Christians can simply channel those desires toward a single woman or man, get married, have kids, join a country club, attend a welcoming church where everything has been designed with people like them in mind, and chase the Jesus-festooned brand of the American dream. . . . Maybe the calling to gay Christian celibacy stands in twenty-first-century America as a precious reminder of just how desperately, helplessly devoted we were meant to be to the cross of Christ. A reminder that every sacrifice we make will pale in comparison to the sacrifice made on our behalf. Maybe the problem isn't that faith costs some of us too much, but that it costs all of us too little.

Gregory Coles[1]

In this chapter, we want to relay a vision for how gay Christians can *reorient* the church. We have intentionally chosen this word because we believe it involves a shift from the typical approach of the church over the past three decades. In the past, the primary approach of the church toward gay individuals has been to make gay people straight, to "reorient" them toward the "correct" sexual orientation. We acknowledge that many individuals have experienced that "reorientation," and that testimonies exist of those who have experienced a shift in their same-sex sexuality. But in this chapter, we want to focus on those Christians with same-sex attractions who do not or have not experienced such a shift. Instead, their experience is that of an enduring same-sex sexuality. In particular, we want to ask how celibate gay Christians can bring their gifts to the church and whether there are even benefits to being gay and living a celibate lifestyle, benefits that can strengthen the body of Christ. Rather than seeking to "reorient" our celibate gay brothers and sisters, we want to ask how their experience of costly obedience to Jesus Christ in our contemporary culture might "reorient" the church in healthy and necessary ways.

To frame this conversation, we ask you to imagine when you first became a Christian. Imagine that early on in your faith you are asked to lead a Bible study for new Christians. You aren't adequately prepared for this ministry, but the need is clear, and so you accept the invitation. *How hard could it be?* you think. After several weeks, you discover that a couple of gay Christians have been attending the study. One night, after everyone else has gone home, they ask you about the implications of the gospel for them, for their sexuality, and for their lives. As a relatively new Christian, you have a few ideas, but you quickly realize that you really aren't sure what the gospel means for a person who is gay. What do you do? Rather than guess at an answer or offer them some initial, speculative thoughts, you decide to write to a well-known Christian to seek his advice.

This scenario—or at least something very close to it—actually happened. Jean Vanauken (her nickname was "Davy") had become a Christian as an adult, and her husband, Sheldon, soon followed Jean into the Christian faith. Shortly after their conversion, they were asked to lead a Bible study for new Christians, and some of the members of the study came to ask them about homosexuality and faith, so they wrote to C. S. Lewis, asking for advice. Lewis wrote back, and this is the only place we know of where Lewis wrote about the topic of homosexuality and same-sex attraction.

In his reply, Lewis compared same-sex desire to other enduring realities that might prevent a person from being able to marry. The best response to such a circumstance, Lewis proposed, was to try to help the person find a vocation in their hardship, to tie their experience to transcendent reality in a way in which God could be glorified. Here is an excerpt from Lewis's letter to Sheldon and Davy:

> First, to map out the boundaries within which all discussion must go on, I take it for certain that the physical satisfaction of homosexual desires is sin. This leaves the homosexual no worse off than any normal person who is, for whatever reason, prevented from marrying. Second, our speculations on the cause of the abnormality are not what matters and we must be content with ignorance. The disciples were not told why (in terms of efficient cause) the man was born blind (John 9:1–3): only the final cause, that the works of God should be made manifest in him. This suggests that in homosexuality, as in every other tribulation, those works can be made manifest: i.e. that every disability conceals a vocation, if only we can find it, which will "turn the necessity to glorious gain."[2]

Later in the letter, C. S. Lewis recalled a letter from "a pious male homosexual" about what that person thought of his own gifts and talents. The following is an excerpt of what Lewis wrote:

What should the positive life of the homosexual be? I wish I had a letter which a pious male homosexual, now dead, once wrote to me—but of course it was the sort of letter one takes care to destroy. He believed that his necessity *could* be turned to spiritual gain: that there were certain kinds of sympathy and understanding, a certain social role which mere *men* and mere *women* could not give. But it is all horribly vague and long ago. Perhaps any homosexual who humbly accepts his cross and puts himself under Divine guidance will, however, be shown the way. . . . All I have really said is that, like all other tribulations, it must be offered to God and His guidance how to use it must be sought.[3]

In this chapter, we will explore in greater detail the "spiritual gain" Lewis writes about. To be clear, we are not speaking of the spiritual gain a gay person receives because of their orientation—though that is also important and a worthwhile topic for discussion. Rather, we want to focus on the spiritual gain the church receives by the presence and the giftings of celibate gay Christians in its midst as active and contributing members of Christ's body. Here is the "reorientation" we spoke of earlier: rather than thinking of gay Christians solely as a group that receives ministry—something true of all of us—we want to shift to the other direction to think about the valuable contributions celibate gay Christians bring to the church as equal colaborers in Christ.

I (Mark) wrote previously about a season of hardship many years ago when I received a letter from a family member. This individual wrote to provide some wisdom on how troubles can lead to our spiritual growth and benefit:

What does it mean to *test* faith? Trials (troubles) test our faith. Why? Because they cause us to question God's promises. They undermine our confident assurance that those things we've not yet seen are going to happen. We've not yet seen them, and this awful thing that's happening to me now makes me wonder if I ever *will* see them.

Yet it is at *this* point that endurance comes into the picture—what is endurance? What is its relationship to faith? If we no longer have confident assurance about things we cannot see, if we are haunted by doubt, or if we are simply so weary or in so much anguish that the things we cannot see become *unreal* to us, it is endurance that makes us continue on, no matter what. It is, in a sense, a willfully blind obedience to God, a stubborn determination to go on, almost like Jacob wrestling with God and refusing to let go until God blessed him.

It is somewhat difficult to reconcile this with James' admonition to consider trials an opportunity for joy—not *because* of the trial, per se, but because of the opportunity to endure. This is an *opportunity* because it *results* in strong character—in a Christian who is ready for anything. . . .

All of this would seem to imply that a Christian whose faith is never tested would not be much of a Christian at all! In other words, God builds into the Christian life aspects of character development that would *not* be possible . . . outside of a fallen world. Here we *must* face situations in which we are *genuinely* tempted to throw in the towel, so that we can also have the *genuine* opportunity to press on, and in pressing on we gain a victory (even a small victory) of faith, and in doing that we develop our own Christian history, our personal Christian memory, which is an integral part of our individual character. We can see what we've been through and how God brought us through it, and we are all ready to face whatever happens next, not because of ourselves, but because of what God already has done for us and in us.[4]

The metaphor of testing speaks to the experience of the celibate gay Christian, calling them to an embrace of obedience that demands sacrifice. This costly obedience tests one's faith in God's promises. But what is the cost they must pay? For the gay Christian, the cost is more than the choice to refrain from sex in a culture saturated with messages communicating sexual self-actualization. As difficult as that may be, it is something they share in common with persons of a heterosexual orientation as well, those who are called to remain celibate outside of the bonds of marriage. For the gay Christian, celibacy is also costly because of its *ongoing* nature, because it is an *enduring* hardship. What do we mean by this ongoing and enduring aspect of their obedience?

Many Christians in the West face few obvious hardships or tests of faith. In the areas where these Christians do struggle, local churches sometimes appear to be catering to them by overlooking certain sins while calling out the sins that the majority finds easy to avoid. This is not something a pastor will readily admit, but it is more common than we realize. It's not that churches are now claiming that these preferred sins are no longer sinful; rather, there is a sense in which these preferred sins are downplayed significantly, to the weakening of the body of Christ. We might hear messages such as "boys will be boys" (which can justify heterosexual lust or adultery), or "blessings accrue to the faithful" (which can justify selfish ambition, greed, covetousness, and economic exploitation), or "just praying for those in our faith community" (which can justify gossip), or similar messages justifying other areas of sin. Yet these same justifications are rarely applied to same-sex sexuality and sexual behavior. This is what Greg Coles referred to in the epigraph that opened this chapter: "Maybe the problem isn't that faith costs some of us too much, but that it costs all of us too little."

Is the solution to water down our expectations for gay Christians? To find ways of accommodating their sin as we have for the heterosexual sin we have "normalized" or that we avoid confronting? Certainly not. We believe the costly obedience of gay celibate Christians has the potential to push the church in the opposite direction, toward greater faithfulness to Christ. Instead of looking down on celibate gay Christians because of their experience as a sexual minority, those of us whose faith doesn't appear very costly should learn to mirror the costly obedience we see modeled by these individuals. When celibate gay Christians commit themselves, however imperfectly, to a path of costly obedience, they are aware of the nature of the commitment they are making—one that may not be resolved in this lifetime, one that may require an enduring faithfulness and persistent sacrifice. They are also aware of the benefits of such obedience, that through this testing God builds up their Christian character in a way that leads to greater spiritual maturity. This commitment to a disciplined and costly discipleship is a strength: a gift that others in the church are called to emulate.

These gifts can be a blessing to the larger body of Christ in several specific ways. Let's consider a few themes that emerge as we consider the experiences of celibate gay Christians. The first two are an extension of what we just mentioned regarding the development and maturing of Christian character. The lives of gay celibate Christians who embrace this costly obedience, embodying gospel teaching on suffering and grace, provide an outward witness of faithfulness to Christ to the surrounding culture.

EMBODYING TEACHING ON SUFFERING AND GRACE

We previously mentioned Henri Nouwen, a Catholic priest and beloved author whose books have been a source of encouragement to countless followers of Christ. To his close friends, Nouwen was known to struggle with same-sex sexuality, and a recently published book of letters on the spiritual life contains a letter Nouwen wrote to a friend about the spiritual significance of his own pain:

I am still quite anxious, I still have real attacks of anguish and sleeping is still a real problem. But I am quite, quite aware that this pain is given to me to purify my heart, to deepen my love for Jesus and to give Him every inch of my being. Whereas in the past the anguish seemed quite disruptive and often paralyzing, now I experience it a little more as a severe companion who wants to show me the narrow road. Once I have found that road and walk safely on it, the anguish might leave me, but right now I am trying simply to accept what the Lord gives me and trust that He knows when, how and where to give me new peace and new joy.[5]

A significant theological tradition looks at the reality of suffering and how Christians can find meaning and purpose in their suffering insofar as they identify with the cross of Christ. St. Joseph of Cupertino wrote, "The adversities and tribulations of life are special graces, and those most to be desired. God reserves them for His clearest friends. Receive them, then, as such with patience, constancy, and joy."[6] The Roman Catholic Church has a robust history of reflecting on this spiritual truth; however, we have found that some Protestants, including many evangelicals, tend to be more comfortable focusing on physical, emotional, and spiritual *healing* rather than considering the spiritual healing or spiritual gain to be found when physical or emotional healing does not take place.

It is this experience of *grace amid suffering*, rather than immediate healing, that many celibate gay Christians will bear witness to. Our interviewee Charles told us how he experiences suffering as a grace from God:

I think that the biggest benefit [of] any story of any Christian who suffers or who has struggles, is that suffering isn't actually punishment from God, that suffering is actually often like a grace from God. It is how he brings us closer to him. I think that also the story of gay celibate Christians is maybe just a powerful message to the world that Jesus Christ is enough.

In Christianity, some have distinguished between joy and pleasure. They define pleasure as a more fleeting experience—certain activities that bring a temporary feeling—while speaking of joy as an enduring reality. Every person longs for joy, and the early Christians wrote less about pleasure than they did about the more enduring nature of joy.[7] We are fully alive when we are most joyful. The supreme human calling is a calling to endless joy, that is, eternal life. But joy, properly understood, is also associated with enduring hardship. In other words, our capacity for joy is tied to our experience of pain that is endured. It is our capacity to endure that enables us to experience joy itself as enduring: "Joy is lasting, like the excellence, the virtues, that engender it. Sense pleasure is individual, like sensation itself. . . . Joy is communicable; it grows by being shared and repays sacrifices freely embraced. Joy belongs to the purity and generosity of love."[8]

Charles, the celibate gay Christian we cited above, unpacked several of the implications of joy as he has seen it manifested in his experience of sexuality:

> You know, the only way that a celibate gay Christian could ever be joyful is for Jesus to actually be who he says that he is. For him to actually be enough to give you what you need to live life. . . . I think that is an amazing testimony to the gospel, that you are not just this bitter person, white-knuckling it, and gritting their teeth, and denying themselves, but that you are someone who is actually fulfilled, and reaching outward, and looking to other people, and you don't seem bitter, and yet you're single and you're not having sex. Like, how can that be?

As Charles's story indicates, his enduring hardship, expressed as hope "for Jesus to actually be who he says that he is," can be an occasion for joy. Yet this hope in the sufficiency of what Jesus promises does not necessarily make the experience of hardship itself less difficult. Enduring hardship also serves as a reminder to set realistic expectations for how people live out their faith. This point was stressed by our interviewee Lucas: "I'm really hesitant to offer people false expectations. I think it's important to be honest about the difficulties of Christian discipleship." In other words, we don't want to offer false hope—we must be honest about the struggle.

Similarly, Charles told us how he has come to understand brokenness and redemption:

> I think that is the power of the cross . . . that God wanted to enter the broken world to begin changing it from the bottom up, piece by piece. So the fact that there is brokenness is not an indictment against God. To me, the fact that there is brokenness is a reminder of the call, or is a huge sign that we need [the] redemption that God brings, that we need the change that God offers, the healing and the restoration that he brings to the world.

Charles sees his ongoing experience of brokenness as a reminder of his need for the power and redemption of God. Later in his interview, Charles elaborated further on how his own testimony of God's provision has been a source of encouragement (and perhaps, at times, a source of challenge) to other Christians:

> I think, like, more than anything, I have experienced this: other people being like, "Wow, it is an amazing testimony that Jesus can be more than I ever thought that he could be." I don't know, I don't think that is why I am doing it, but I think that is part of . . . the effect that it has on people when

they hear the stories of gay celibate Christians . . . that Jesus can be more than a lot of people give him credit for, or even try to allow him to be.

Charles spoke of the testimonial nature of his obedience, that the sufficiency he finds in his costly obedience to Christ is a clear pointer to Jesus. But what this cannot mean for the body of Christ is that celibate gay Christians live out this costly obedience and the rest of the church is unmoved by the cost. Rather, we see this as an invitation to the church to receive as a gift the opportunity to learn from these brothers and sisters while also offering them the grace of God in full relationship with one another. What we are suggesting is that the costly obedience of celibate gay Christians should impact the full church by being a model of what we are all called to live into: a life of sacrifice in which the hardships we face are given meaning and significance in relation to the passion of Christ. And the church needs to consider what it means to share in that cost.

Making a church community a place of support, open communication, planned fellowship, and relationship building requires intentionality and effort. It's easy to write out a monthly check to the church, thinking your work done. We believe the church has been content with this level of involvement with the gay community. What is needed now is the more difficult choice of emotional engagement with people who are different but who share a similar desire to walk with Christ. Opening your heart to the unknown and investing in a relationship that might not look all that appealing in the beginning can be risky. We believe, however, that such relationships within the body of Christ have the potential to become more rewarding than others because of the depth, authenticity, and support they require. By investing deeply in relationships with celibate gay Christians, the entire church has an opportunity to witness true transformational power by walking together with these individuals through their ongoing journey.

We are aware that those who are single and heterosexual might feel that their own costly obedience is a similar hardship. We are not in any way suggesting otherwise. If it helps to think in this way, we could consider celibate gay Christians as a subset of a larger population of single Christians. That said, we do not want to minimize the unique challenges they face as well, in terms of how sexual identity and the cultural discourse on sex and gender norms have shaped and challenged their journey of discipleship. The best way we can say this is that no experience of costly obedience is identical, but neither is anyone excluded from the invitation to journey on this discipleship path.

A DELIGHTFUL INHERITANCE
Greg Coles

A few weeks ago in a meeting I was attending, our leader asked for a volunteer to retrieve supplies from a nearby storage closet. His exact words were "if someone would be willing to go into the closet. . . ."

There was a long, smirk-and-chuckle-laden pause as we all pondered the double entendre of his words. And then I melodramatically burst out, "But I just got out of there!"

If you had told me five years ago that present-day Greg would make that joke in public, I wouldn't have believed you. If you had told me that I would find joy and delight within my vocation as a celibate gay follower of Jesus, that I would talk about faith and sexuality to near-strangers at full volume with a smile on my face, I would have asked which mind-altering recreational pharmaceutical you were smoking.

The only way I knew to talk about gay celibacy in those days—the only way I knew to think about it—was with funereal sorrow. I was convinced that my unabating attraction to the same sex, and my lack of attraction to the opposite sex, had rendered me a second-string disciple of Jesus. I couldn't rise to the big leagues in the kingdom of God until I developed a sexual desire for women. In the meantime, whatever joys I discovered as a celibate person would never be more than consolation prizes, cheap trinkets given in lieu of marriage's far better rewards.

But in these last five years, though my gay orientation has remained immobile, my orientation toward mourning has been metamorphosing more and more into an occasion for joy. Here are a few of the epiphanies that diminished my shame over being gay and expanded my joy:

1. The opportunity to resist sexual temptation by the grace of God, to receive forgiveness when I stumble, and to steward my sexuality in holy ways is no less available to me than it is to every other follower of Jesus, gay and straight alike.

2. As a gay man, I experience absolutely no temptation to lust after my sisters in Christ—thus, there is a kind of sexual holiness that comes more easily to me than it does to most other men. I can enjoy relationships with women free from the expectation or fear of sexualization.

3. Based on my experience of sexuality and my beliefs about sexual ethics, my calling to celibacy feels abundantly clear. Instead of feeling angst and uncertainty about whether or when I ought to get married, I can throw myself headlong into singleness.

4. If I take seriously what the apostle Paul wrote in 1 Corinthians 7, the vocation of celibacy is not inferior to the vocation of marriage in the eyes of God—in fact, it provides a unique set of opportunities.

5. Relational intimacy is not exclusive to marriage. We can experience rich, life-giving intimacy with our fellow journeyers and colaborers in Christ, even and especially when our obedience to Christ causes us to say no to other forms of intimacy.

To be clear, not everything about gay celibacy fills me with giddy exuberance. My life, like any human life, is full of challenge and brokenness, parts of which have a lot to do with my sexuality. My celibacy inspires particular stresses and sorrows—just as marriage lends itself to another set of stresses and sorrows (or so my married friends tell me). And in today's polarized world, being a gay celibate follower of Jesus means I stand in the crossfire of a handful of religious and political skirmishes, too sympathetic to each warring camp to fully belong in either one.

There are times—there will probably always be times—when I need to mourn my circumstances as a celibate gay person. When those times come, I pray for grace to mourn well and for companions to mourn alongside me.

And yet, to the extent that I bring my challenge and brokenness to Jesus and say yes to his invitation, I find delight in the particular, unremarkable story that happens to be mine. I learn to exclaim with glee alongside David in Psalm 16:6, "The boundary lines have fallen for me in pleasant places; surely I have a delightful inheritance."

A MORE HONEST DISCUSSION
ABOUT SEXUALITY

Ironically, one of the potential benefits of this shift in the church is that it may lead to more open and sincere discussion about sexuality and sexual behavior in general. Sex is not a topic Christians have historically been comfortable discussing, and we find in much of our research that few people would say their church ever discussed sexuality. The reality of people experiencing sexual desires that they are called to abstain from is not unique to celibate gay Christians, as Jean observed:

> People around me make a way bigger deal about being gay, but for some reason, the more that I grapple with it, the less of a big deal it is and the more it's just my personal brand of creating an experience that has never been perfect or without something twisted about it. Everyone's sexuality has something twisted about it. . . . Even if they never had sex outside of marriage, married somebody of the opposite sex and never had an affair. . . . There's brokenness there, so it's helped to realize that. . . .
>
> But, yeah, I think I can help other people around me to . . . come to a realization that their sexuality is broken too. I don't think it's my job to go out there and tell everyone they're messed up. I just think, like it or not, we have that in common. . . . I don't think it's going to just come naturally for other people. I don't think most straight Christians in the church consider that a lot of times their marriage is broken, too, that their sexuality is broken too.

One way in which gay celibate Christians are a gift to the church is in how God is using them to open the door to more honest discussion about sexuality. Whether we join Jean in framing sexuality as "broken," whether we think of C. S. Lewis's language of "tribulation" or "necessity" or "a cross," or whether we adopt a more optimistic framework like that of "stewarding sexual desire," we have many examples of words and categories that could lead us toward a better and more open conversation—a conversation that cuts across married and single, gay and straight, toward some fundamental principles for living with challenging circumstances we all face in and through our sexuality.

OUTWARD WITNESS TO CONTEMPORARY CULTURE

We recently heard a pastor speaking about the need for young adults in the church to bring clean water to villages in Africa. Acts like these tangibly express faith in Christ by making a real, felt difference in people's lives. The pastor went on to note that the broader society in which we live will applaud noble pursuits like this. Now take those same young adults and challenge them to live out a countercultural sexual ethic, one that rubs against the grain of what society finds acceptable today. Our broader culture will not know how to evaluate what they are doing. They may be pitied or patronized. But they will almost certainly not be applauded.

Christians are called to live countercultural lives. Yet much of contemporary Christianity in the West cannot not be described as "countercultural." Instead, the witness of the church has been diluted by compromise with the broader culture. Sadly, there are times when Western Christianity even lags behind secular Western culture in reflecting the radical welcome of Jesus. The countercultural witness of the Christian faith has not been clear and evident in recent years.

We raise this point to highlight the radical, countercultural nature of the commitment gay Christians make in living celibate.

As they embrace the path of costly obedience, their lives naturally attract attention and raise questions. Alex shared the following: "A major benefit [of gay Christian celibacy] is being a challenge to society. It's just something that's very radical. The fact that you're not getting married, the fact that you're not having sex . . . celibacy is a very countercultural thing. Living against the grain of culture." Charles, another interviewee, agreed: "I feel like our story can shout back to that world, like, 'Actually, life isn't about being happy. Life is about glorifying God and making much in him, and when we do that, we actually find a deep, deep joy which is way more powerful and way more satisfying than any sort of happiness.' And also, 'Christ is enough.'"

AS A SOURCE OF CRITIQUE— IRON SHARPENS IRON

Christian leaders are frequently on the defense, seeking to explain the biblical doctrines and teaching on gender and sexual ethics. Traditional teaching on marriage, sexuality, and sexual behavior is frequently dismissed and characterized as "bigotry," "bias," "prejudice," and "anti-gay." In response, some Christians develop a fairly thick skin and no longer listen to the critique of those who do not share their sexual ethics. Unfortunately, that thick skin may also prevent Christians from hearing legitimate critiques and making adjustments in their approach to sexual identity and ministry.

This is where we see exceptional value in encouraging discussion between church leaders and the gay celibate community. What if the source of the critique of the church and its sexual ethic was not an LGBTQ+ activist, whose goals include changing church doctrine or undermining normative parameters for sexual intimacy? What if, instead, the source of the critique was a fellow follower of Christ whose experience of same-sex sexuality puts them in a unique position to inform church leadership about how the church itself can be experienced by people dealing with sexual-identity issues in their lives?

Lucas reported the following: "Because I accept the traditional church teaching, it is easier to hear from me rather than someone who is gay and challenging the church teaching, but I also think I can do a lot to humanize the issue for them and help them to see people on the other side in more human terms."

We believe there is a missed opportunity here. A gay Christian who is living faithfully before God can provide feedback to the church that might be rejected out of hand were it to come from someone who is a gay activist or apologist, actively antagonistic to the church or the Christian faith. Some insights about how the church can grow—insights for improving church climate, growing in compassion, and upholding the value of singleness—may be heard and received when they come from celibate gay Christians.

A related benefit celibate gay Christians bring to the body of Christ is that they add a missing element of diversity, one that might otherwise be overlooked. This diversity is a source of critique for some insofar as the church tends to think of itself as reflecting a single, uniform way of being in the world, one race or ethnicity, or a specific presentation of itself that functionally applies only to those who are "just like me." Sebastian made this comment:

> I don't think straight people hear themselves talk very often, especially conservative straight people—they have no clue. I remember growing up hearing that AIDS was a scourge on the homosexual. It was like Old Testament comes to roost. It was like, *They are out there, and they are not in here.* Of course, it's fine to talk this way instead of realizing that there are [gay] people in here. Even if we are only like 2 to 3 percent of the population, we still are in here. I like to tell my story so they can hear what I hear, so they can get a little of

a taste for the anxiety I grew up with. I think also it is good for people to hear from people who are not like them in the church, whether it's a different race or ethnicity or a different country.

HUMANIZING THE ISSUE

In addition to helping Christians develop a receptivity to constructive critique, knowing celibate gay Christians can humanize a topic that is frequently reduced to an "issue" or a set of policies or a legislative win or loss. LGBTQ+ issues have been central in the "culture wars" for many years now. It is all too easy to allow this clash of attitudes, values, and public policies to eclipse the persons who are represented by such policies. There is a risk that churches that embrace the culture wars will be predisposed to see the LGBTQ+ community as an abstract enemy rather than as a group of human beings loved by God.

Celibate gay Christians bring to the body of Christ a humanizing of the topic, making the abstract real. Recall how Lucas said that in addition to saying things that can be heard by fellow Christians, he can also "do a lot to humanize the issue for [fellow Christians]." Lucas went on to say how improving cultural engagement can impact the gospel's reach in the public square:

> I think, at least, I can help Christians to be better peacemakers and . . . not to be inflaming things more than they have. And I think what tends to get lost in all the culture wars stuff is the fact that a huge number of people within the church who are sexual minorities . . . aren't getting good pastoral care. And so my story can help remind the church that being there and showing love to people is more important than cultural conflict that pushes people away from the gospel. Not that I think there is no place for people in the public square, but we

want to make sure that what we do in the public square is not pushing people away from Christ.

Ben shared his hope "that somehow I could use my story to be an educational experience for people who aren't really familiar with this. To help them think more individually, more personally. That it's not just about them, but it's an us and us kind of conversation. That it's not us that are better but it's us, here, all at the table together."

Every celibate gay Christian we interviewed would have appreciated knowing that there were older men and women like them, people who also navigated same-sex sexuality and found a path where they could flourish, who found a church where they could use their gifts and talents. Some of our interviewees discussed how they have tried to become such a resource to others like themselves. For example, Charles explained the sense of purposefulness he feels as he shares his story with others:

> [I] especially [enjoy] meeting with or kind of informally counseling a lot of younger guys in my church, who are also primarily to exclusively same-sex attracted and are also convinced that it is not in the Lord's will to act on that, or who are at least seeking or interested in acting on that position. I just thought, *Oh wow, the things that I have been through, the experiences I have, are really meaningful and life-giving to these guys*, and . . . I was able to experience my life as a same-sex-attracted but still single Christian as, like, an opportunity to bless other people, so it has taken on more of a positive identity for me."

Charles went on to say, "I think . . . one day my story could get heard by the youth of the church, or similar stories to mine, just to give kids an alternative narrative than that which they [hear from] either conservative Christians or the world about their sexuality."

ATTUNED TO THE MARGINS

Another spiritual gain that celibate gay Christians can bring to the church is a heightened sensitivity to those who might be on the margins of society, the underserved, the down-and-out. While this sensitivity is certainly valuable to ministry among the LGBTQ+ community, it also extends beyond that discussion to the varied experiences of people who may be struggling and wondering what the church has to offer them in their difficult circumstances. Charles shared from his experience:

> If it hadn't been for this long, drawn-out experience of suffering and processing suffering and what that is like . . . I wouldn't have at all been able to relate to marginalized people or people who are really lost and alone in a lifelong battle with sexual-identity struggle or crisis. And I just can see, like I see people who struggle with alcoholism or with eating disorders, and with minorities who feel like their stories are marginalized or erased. . . . And I have found that many times it is really my experience of my spirituality that gives me the compassion, and often it gives me some sort of way into the conversation, or some sort of way that I can begin to have empathy for people. And I really think that it has made me so much softer and compassionate and really given me the heart of Christ.

Charles added later that sometimes pastors seek him out for his opinion on approaches to reaching and serving those on the margins. Of course, there is no guarantee that the broader church will be receptive to the message that we need to care for those on the margins, but to have people for whom such a call to ministry resonates is a true and beautiful gift to the body of Christ.

Alex shared, "If I had no minority status at all, I don't think I would be—[I] wouldn't have that empathy for marginalized people if I wasn't marginalized." Alex told us a little later in his interview how being gay can lead to greater authenticity and reflect that a church community is open to dialogue: "I think that having that kind of voice for people of my age is helpful. I would help that. It would increase the diversity by the fact that I am gay. . . . Not just gay people but any person who comes feels welcomed, feels authentic."

TIME TO INVEST IN MINISTRY

Another practical gift that many celibate gay Christians bring to the church is time to invest in others through ministry. While it is not uniformly true that single people have more time for ministry than married couples, the apostle Paul suggested that freedom to use time to serve the Lord is one benefit of the single life. In 1 Corinthians 7:32–35 Paul wrote why it might be good to remain single:

> But I want you to be free from concern. One who is unmarried is concerned about the things of the Lord, how he may please the Lord; but one who is married is concerned about the things of the world, how he may please his wife, and his interests are divided. The woman who is unmarried, and the virgin, is concerned about the things of the Lord, that she may be holy both in body and spirit; but one who is married is concerned about the things of the world, how she may please her husband. This I say for your own benefit; not to put a restraint upon you, but to promote what is appropriate and to secure undistracted devotion to the Lord. (NASB)

Celibate gay Christians remind us to have a high view of singleness rather than idolizing marriage. Charles related something that resonates with the spirit of Paul:

And not only compassion on others, but I feel like I have . . . margin in my life to listen to them. Like if I were living the traditional sort of Christian narrative, then I would be married and have kids at my age. There's a lot that I—a lot of stories that I would have never been able to hear, a lot of lives that I would have never been able to engage with, or live into, some people I would have never gotten to learn from. So I feel like not only has it changed the quality of the way that I have been able to interact with Christians, but it has given me some degree of quantity, of more space and more relational energy than [most] people have or than I would have otherwise had to spend time with other Christians at the church. So that has been really important to me.

Alex also cited the apostle Paul and 1 Corinthians 7 regarding time and resources. "Celibacy points toward a heavenly reality," he said. In his view, unmarried people have the opportunity of "just being more available for people" and having "more time to give to more people." Reflecting on the celibate gay Christians he knew, Alex concluded that they were the "most hospitable people I've met," showing him "what it means to be radically hospitable."

Similarly, Jean shared how she has flexibility and capacity that Christians who choose to marry do not have:

[The] benefits are, just by nature of not being married, there's just a lot more capacity for others and for yourself, I mean, honestly. My married friends are notorious for not having a lot of flexibility and free time and carefree moments. I mean, spontaneity—that's not their game. Their game is, "Well, I've made this choice and I've committed to this person, and maybe these children, this family, this unit." . . . When you're single and unattached, there's new ways you can be used. You know, maybe in vocational ministry, you could just far exceed because you're called to that first and foremost, and not a family unit first and foremost. And I think that's huge in light of the gay issue.

This capacity, this bandwidth, can also dramatically shift a person's self-perception. For example, Charles identified a shift from "shame-based" to "opportunity-based" ways of looking at his experiences and his availability:

[A positive view of my singleness] seemed to actually transform . . . a shame-based feeling about my sexual orientation into almost more of an opportunity-based feeling. That as a single person, you have a lot more energy, that you can form more relationships, and you can do more good—form more, kind of, investments in the local church than would otherwise be true if I were a married person.

INCREASED AUTHENTICITY

Some celibate gay Christians felt they could bring the gift of greater honesty and transparency to the church. Questions about difficult topics or about the hardships of life so often go unasked (and unanswered) unless someone is willing to break the silence by being honest about their own challenges and doubts. Desmond told us this:

I have observed that when I share honestly and authentically, people say they get a lot out of it. Exactly why that's the case, I can't completely vouch for. I think maybe it's because I'm honest about things that a lot of other people find uncomfortable or taboo. Not necessarily in terms of my sex life but more in the sense of being honest about the frustrations and difficulties of trying to follow God. In a lot of

Christian circles, it's unacceptable to be honest about that kind of thing, and it can lead to an extremely oppressive atmosphere, and it makes it impossible to be open to yourself or to God about yourself. I'm deeply convinced that no matter how unpleasant it is, honesty is the first necessity of following God. That literally nothing can be done without that. Because without that, you're not dealing with family.

When C. S. Lewis wrote to Sheldon and Davy Vanauken, he discussed how the pious homosexual man he mentioned had described his capacity for "certain kinds of sympathy and understanding" that might not be as readily accessible to others. We are not sure how to describe this capacity, nor are we suggesting that heterosexual Christians cannot have such a capacity. But we are asking whether there is greater societal opportunity to locate sympathy and understanding—and perhaps other emotions and ways of relating—in and among gay people, in a way that is good for the church, that could be "turned to spiritual gain."

CULTIVATING CLOSE FRIENDSHIPS

Henri Nouwen once wrote to a friend about their friendship and how it had become a source of sadness to him in part because it could not "blossom and deepen":

I honestly do not want anything more or less than a good solid loving friendship. It is important for me to express to you at times my feelings and emotions and my affective struggles. There are few people to whom I let myself be known in that way, and when I am with you there is a certain hope that you will give me some extra space to be with you as a friend who does not have to hide much. But the last few times I felt so much distance and so much resistance to be with me where I am needy that I wondered if it would be wise for me to pursue our friendship. I don't want to be in pain every time I leave you. Nor do I want you to feel guilty or simply frustrated. . . .

What I keep hoping for are friends who protect, support and care for my celibate choice while not withholding from me a nurturing affective friendship that allows me to shed some tears of loneliness from time to time and return to the "battlefield" knowing that I have friends who support me.[9]

Friendships with gay celibate church members are investments on the part of heterosexual church members, investments that require time and emotional engagement. Yet they are necessary if we are serious about building bindings or "supporting ligaments" that hold the church together (Eph 4:1–16). Thanks in large part to the experience and work of celibate gay Christians, the topic of friendship has received more attention in recent years. Wesley Hill is coeditor with Ron Belgau of *Spiritual Friendship*, a blog that places great emphasis on the role of friendship in the lives of those living as celibate gay Christians. In a blog post titled "The Ministry Gay Christians Have," Hill wrote,

It struck me today that perhaps what we're doing here at Spiritual Friendship could be captured in the ambiguity of that word "ministry." Yes, we want gay people who are lonely and hurting to find sheltered spaces where they can receive forgiveness, the binding up of wounds, and the comfort needed to go on hoping. We want them to be ministered *to*. But we also—and perhaps even more prominently—want gay people who are in Christ to follow their callings, impart their stories, offer their insights, and exercise the full range of their gifts in the church and for the sake of the world. We want them to *do the work of ministry.*

Hill continued, "A wise Christian mentor said to a group of us recently that perhaps many celibate gay Christians have (among other gifts) a particular genius for cultivating and sustaining close friendships. If so, that can be understood as a *ministry*—not so much anyone's ministry to us but our ministry to *others*. It's a ministry we are called to and equipped to perform, not simply a ministry we receive."[10]

When a ministry of friendship is lived out within the body of Christ, it has the capacity not only to build and deepen individual friendships but also to build and deepen the sense of *community* within our church communities. In his interview, Charles reflected on this theme: "[My] hope, what is most important to me, the most healthy place to be in, is to be the kind of person who helps create community."

CONCLUSION

In this chapter, we have sought to turn the concept of "change" around by asking whether, in fact, celibate gay Christians can reorient the body of Christ. Perhaps these brothers and sisters are uniquely equipped to bear witness to Christian values that have eroded in the church, particularly in the West. We considered whether celibate gay Christians have had a unique experience of costly obedience, one that leads to strengthened character and other virtues that may be of great benefit to the church today. We listened to celibate gay Christians tell what they see as some of their potential contributions to the church.

As we have seen throughout this book, there exists a disconnect between the underlying assumptions of Christian pastors regarding same-sex sexuality and expectations of change or healing, imprecision with respect to language for framing pastoral care, and the corresponding church climate and the experiences and needs of celibate gay Christians. Indeed, celibate gay Christians resonate with elements of what we referred to as a gay script and communal dimensions of the LGBTQ+ community, particularly as these elements contrast sharply with experiences in the church. On the other hand, celibate gay Christians reject other elements of the gay script, such as same-sex sexual behavior, in an effort to live faithfully in response to what they believe is God's call on their lives. This dynamic presents a complicated relationship for celibate gay Christians and the church and the LGBTQ+ community that requires pastors, priests, elders, deacons, and other Christian leaders to develop cultural competence, pursue wisdom and discernment, and offer more nuance than what is frequently encountered at present.

This disconnect has led us away from creating a church that is intentionally relational, formational, and secure, which is what is needed to form the kinds of relationships that would support the costly obedience gay celibate Christians are called to if they wish to live faithful to Christ. Friends who function as family to celibate gay Christians provide several models for what it could look like to establish and maintain relationships. Ironically, celibate gay Christians may be the very people whose unique ministry could enrich the church in many ways, including the fostering of greater authenticity and depth of relationships.

Celibate gay Christians have at times been treated as sinners to be confronted, embarrassments to be hidden away, liabilities to be managed, or charity cases to be ministered to. We are hopeful, however, that churches will increasingly come to see the celibate gay Christians in their midst as spiritual peers and colaborers in the gospel, people who bring precious and unique gifts to the body of Christ, people designed to minister as well as to be ministered to. We hope that heterosexual Christians who have previously been fearful or suspicious will come to honor the costly obedience of the celibate gay Christians journeying alongside them.

FOR DISCUSSION

1. Which of the potential contributions that celibate gay Christians identified strikes you as most important for the church in the West today? Why? How does this chapter help you articulate your appreciation for someone who struggles with self-acceptance and life purpose as discussed in chapter 3?

2. What is the cost of building close friendships in the church that foster the development of "supporting ligaments"? How do you think those could be encouraged on the individual and church levels in your faith community?

3. What do you see as the remaining obstacles hindering the church from seeing celibate gay Christians as having something of great value to bring to the church today? What suggestions do you have for how those obstacles might be overcome?

4. Where do you think the discussion should go from here? What are the next steps for you? For your local faith community?

CONCLUSION

As we bring this book to a close, we want to reflect on what we have learned from studying celibate gay Christians. We also want to acknowledge readers who may be digesting this new information or feeling challenged with a new point of view and raising objections. Finally, we want to discuss some "next steps" to continue engaging the conversation.

WHAT HAVE WE LEARNED?

What have we learned about celibate gay Christians? We learned, first, that celibacy is defined rather broadly by Side B gay Christians. Some view celibacy as a lifelong commitment to abstain from sexual relationships. Others view celibacy as a commitment to abstain from sexual relationships at this time but also to remain open to a relationship with the opposite sex or to abstain from same-sex relationships but be in a relationship with someone of the opposite sex, which some refer to as entering a mixed-orientation marriage.

We also learned that celibate gay Christians report varying degrees of same-sex and opposite-sex attraction and are highly religious. Their religiosity is present in their behavior (church attendance and religious practices, such as prayer) and also in their desire to carry their faith into all aspects of their lives.

They value their identity as Christians first and foremost. Some use the term "celibate gay Christian" or otherwise value the use of the word "gay" to describe themselves, while others do not place the same amount of weight or significance on these terms in describing themselves. They agree that same-sex sexual behavior is morally impermissible. There is less consensus about whether being attracted to the same sex is itself morally impermissible. They tend not to believe that people have a say in whether they experience same-sex attraction, often reflecting that they may be biologically predisposed to same-sex attractions. They are not in agreement about whether experience or the environment plays more of a role than biology. Most of our celibate gay Christians do not believe people can change their attractions to the same sex. They do view celibacy as a viable option.

We were perhaps most surprised to learn that on measures of depression, anxiety, and stress, as well as well-being, our sample is doing better than expected. Most were in the normal range for depression, anxiety, and stress, and on another measure of distress, most again scored in the normal range. On a measure of well-being, most of our sample scored high on overall life satisfaction. Where they tended to struggle was in personal relationships, feeling part of their community, and future security. On another measure of personal well-being, our sample scored higher than we might have expected, but where they were low (relative to their other scores) was in self-acceptance. These last few scores mirrored an interesting finding on adult attachment in which the highest percentage of respondents were identified as having a preoccupied attachment style. This suggests that when they experience threats and their attachment system is activated, they can feel preoccupied and anxious about relationships. These feelings create opportunities for others to express genuine care and encouragement in sustained relationships.

Unfortunately, the local church culture may be too precarious for celibate gay Christians to navigate in light of the broader cultural discourse surrounding sexuality and LGBTQ+ concerns and may not be poised to provide the kind of safety and alleviation of fear necessary to establish more secure attachment relationships. We love and pray for pastors and other leaders in the body of Christ. They are called to shepherd those under their care. We want to equip them with information, language, and categories that expand their capacity to shepherd well those who are navigating sexual identity and faith, including those who identify as celibate gay Christians.

We also see celibate gay Christians as having unique experiences and gifts that they can bring to the body of Christ. We do not want Christian leaders to think in terms of "reaching down" to celibate gay Christians, although there are opportunities to create safety and address areas of concern that make it difficult to navigate same-sex sexuality in the church today. Rather, it can be helpful to think of the many ways in which celibate gay Christians may strengthen the church, particularly in areas where the church is not that strong, such as identifying with and reaching those on the margins, fostering greater authenticity and depth in relationships, and valuing singleness.

ADDRESSING OBJECTIONS AND DIGESTING NEW INFORMATION

Perhaps you are still digesting all of this new information and have reservations or even objections about some of the things you have read in this book. As we noted in the preface, the two main objections to celibate gay Christians is that they are not "put[ting] to death the misdeeds of the body" (Rom 8:13) in the way some Christians read Paul in Romans 8. That is, they equate putting to death sin with being rid of one's same-sex impulses. The other objection is that believers ought not to identify with their sin.

To be human is to struggle with sin. We all struggle with sin. None of us will be free from that struggle until the consummation of all things upon Christ's return. But different theological traditions emphasize to differing degrees what a person might expect this side of eternity, so we might expect to see some variations here that reflect denominational differences. However, we seem to extend more grace to ongoing struggles with the unique ways in which the fall has touched our lives in some areas but not in others. Perhaps what critics object to is that they do not believe celibate gay Christians are struggling against the fall or against sin or that some even describe good qualities associated with their present state, as when a celibate gay Christian describes being more attuned to deepened friendships because of how central that is to their well-being. Our purpose in this book is not to settle these questions, but we would encourage a higher quality of discussion about these topics and especially how we think about our impulses and how we conceptualize same-sex attractions. From our perspective, those with differing opinions on these topics seem to be speaking past one another. Some church leaders and some celibate gay Christians seem to us, at times, to be describing two different things, rather than disagreeing on precisely the same thing.

A second main objection raised by many who are critical of the celibate gay Christian movement has to do with whether celibate gay Christians are appropriating language from the gay community that is fundamentally incompatible with an identity in Christ. Again, our purpose is not to settle this question here. The discussion extends beyond this book, and we would remind you that not even our sample of celibate gay Christians agrees with one another on the salience of some of this language. Celibate gay Christians differ as to how important specific terms and self-defining attributions are. We are concerned, however, that the way these discussions have become polarized will not allow celibate gay Christians to discuss among themselves the reasons why some favor particular terms while others may see value in them but choose not to use them for one reason or another.

Perhaps the most interesting new information uncovered in our survey is what we have learned about attachment and how local churches might become emotionally and spiritually safe for people who have been casualties of the broader cultural discourse regarding sexuality and sexual behavior. Celibate gay Christians are navigating two different communities: the local faith community that they identify with by virtue of their life in Christ and the mainstream LGBTQ+ community by virtue of their same-sex sexuality. While the LGBTQ+ community offers answers to questions about identity in what we have described as a gay script, what it really provides is a promise of an emotionally safe space to be honest about one's sexuality. In contrast, the local church often struggles to provide an emotionally and spiritually safe place that is comparable to what can be found in the broader LGBTQ+ community. Christians, in an effort to provide care, may at times inadvertently drive people away from the local church and toward the mainstream LGBTQ+ community.

To our fellow Christians who want to lean into a relationship with a celibate gay Christian in their church, we have several suggestions. In recent research on attachment processes, developing trust and intimacy in relationships is a "dynamic process" that starts when a person "reveals personally significant aspects of him- or herself."[1] What happens after that initial revelation is very important. Research shows that "a sensitive, accepting, supportive, and encouraging response facilitates the expression of deeper personal needs and concerns, which gradually leads to the development of an intimate relationship."[2] Unfortunately, many people don't experience this kind of sensitivity and support in their local churches. Even if an individual has unanswered questions about enduring same-sex attractions or isn't sure how to think about them (with respect to biblical interpretations of putting to death sin), these types of questions are best explored in a relationship of trust and mutual respect, with humility rather than from an adversarial posture that portrays itself as safeguarding the sanctity of the church. We believe there is value in engaging in open conversation about these topics rather than in presenting one's conclusions about whether same-sex attractions ought to change or in using self-defining attributions as a canonical, unarguable truth. Christians who wish to enter relationships with celibate gay Christians would do well to enter into those relationships with great humility about experiences that they have not had.

In a church setting, we should seek to convey three things: (1) understanding (Am I conveying that I actually perceive what matters to the person I am listening to?); (2) validation (Am I conveying a respect for the person I am listening to?); and care (Am I conveying that I care about the person's welfare?).[3] Some of the current discussion about language and terms might be improved by moving away from the question of whether or not specific language should be used (as though it were an all-or-nothing proposal for all persons at all ages and in all circumstances). Instead, we believe more fruitful discussion might be focused on the potential benefits and drawbacks of the use of language, identity labels, and so on, and by whom, at different developmental stages and in various contexts. Such discussions might enrich a sense of shared mission and vision and create better dialogue rather than debate.

NEXT STEPS

So what do we suggest are the next steps in this conversation? In the preface we mentioned two conferences in 2018 that took place for the first time. The first was the Revoice conference, which described itself as a conference for "supporting, encouraging, and empowering gay, lesbian, same-sex-attracted, and other LGBT Christians so they can flourish while observing the historic Christian doctrine of marriage and sexuality."[4] The other was a preconference sponsored by Spiritual Friendship, where some of the best writing and reflection on what it means to be a celibate gay Christian is taking place. These conferences are new and significant developments in the effort to create a scaffolding of sorts for people who are living out a costly obedience to Christ as celibate gay Christians. Before these conferences, much of what was available was limited to books and articles and an online presence that was often deep in theological and philosophical reflection but was less focused on the relational components and practical dimensions of support that can be fostered in conferences and other venues.

Unfortunately, conference organizers and attendees saw a strong negative reaction to the conferences. Our hope in writing this book is that we might begin to see more constructive dialogue between fellow Christians of opposing viewpoints. The responses to these conferences were primarily about whether living with enduring same-sex attraction is morally acceptable and whether it is appropriate for a follower of Christ ever to use *gay* as a self-defining attribution.

One response to the criticism came from conference organizer Nate Collins who, in a press release, highlighted common values around sexual behavior and marriage and the salience of the Christian's foundational identity "in Christ":

> To be explicit, we believe that the Bible is the inspired and inerrant Word of God, and that it restricts all sexual behavior to the context of a marriage covenant, which is defined in the Bible as the emotional, spiritual, and physical union of a man and a woman that is ordered toward procreation. Furthermore, we affirm the spiritual reality that the foundation of a Christian's identity is the person and work of Jesus Christ, that Christian identity is centered in the spiritual reality of being "in Christ" (Eph. 2:6), and that one's

224 • Costly Obedience

identity "in Christ" is the result of his or her union with the resurrected Son of God through the supernatural work of the Holy Spirit.

Collins also acknowledged how differences in language may be a concern to some fellow believers:

> We also acknowledge that different Christian faith traditions will use different terminology to describe the manner in which LGBT experience intersects with Christian faith. The terms we use as an organization are, correspondingly, diverse, in order to draw churched, unchurched, and dechurched individuals into conversation about matters related to faith, gender, and sexuality.[5]

In addition, we encourage further dialogue between pastors and other Christian ministry leaders who have reservations or strong objections to certain language and terminology, even those whose theology leads them to conclude that living with enduring same-sex attraction is itself morally impermissible. These kinds of conferences may provide a helpful venue for future discussions about these difficult topics and, we hope, will foster mutual respect among believers who see these issues differently. We recognize that this conversation may be more exhausting for celibate gay Christians, who may at times feel they have little motivation to explain their perspective on language and identity again. But we believe the future for celibate gay Christians must include the local church. We think it would be wise to focus primarily on what is shared in common—namely, a traditional Christian sexual ethic— and to selectively engage on topics where there is disagreement. With the right dialogue partners, opportunities exist to clarify concerns, identify areas of mutual agreement, and model respect as brothers and sisters in Christ.

In our previous work,[6] we noted that at least three broad ministry postures exist today for people navigating same-sex sexuality and faith and who are convicted that same-sex sexual behavior is morally impermissible. One is related to efforts to change orientation, identity, and behavior. This has been the ex-gay narrative. A second approach is to change identity and behavior when orientation has not changed. This is a ministry that often emphasizes one's identity "in Christ" or uses related categories to account for identity and proscribes same-sex behavior. The third posture involves refraining from same-sex sexual behavior in keeping with a traditional Christian ethic while experiencing enduring same-sex attractions, rooting one's walk in Christ, and reflecting greater latitude in terminology. Our hope for today's church is that a day will come when those who hold these three ministry postures will no longer be at war with one another but will pray for one another and acknowledge one another as brothers and sisters in Christ.

NOTES

Foreword

1. Revoice, home page, www.revoice.us/.
2. Alan Chambers, president of Exodus International, panel discussion at the Gay Christian Network annual conference in Orlando, Florida, January 6, 2012.
3. Justin Lee, *Torn: Rescuing the Gospel from the Gays-vs.-Christians Debate* (New York: Jericho, 2012), 238.

Preface

1. Q Christian Fellowship, www.qchristian.org/mission/.
2. Revoice, home page, www.revoice.us/.
3. C. Baker, O. Zaporozhets, M. A. Yarhouse, and M. Newmeyer, "Attachment, Well-Being, Distress, and Spirituality in Celibate Gay Christians" (paper presented at Southern Association for Counselor Education and Supervision 2016 Conference, New Orleans, LA, October 2016); C. Baker, O. Zaporozhets, M. A. Yarhouse, and M. Newmeyer, "Attachment, Well-Being, Distress, and Spirituality in Celibate Gay Christians" (poster presented at the American Counseling Association National Conference, San Francisco, CA, March 2017).
4. M. A. Yarhouse et al., "Pastors' Experiences with and Attitude toward Persons Who Experience Same-Sex Attraction in the Church," in *Understanding Sexuality: Perspectives and Challenges of the 21st Century*, ed. Oskar Enok and Jokum Rolf (New York: Nova Science, 2018), 49–78.

5. M. Nicolas, M. A. Yarhouse, O. Zaporozhets, T. Stauffer, D. Harrell, and C. Hamling, "Friends Who Function as Family to Celibate Gay Christians" (poster presented at the Christian Association for Psychological Studies National Conference, Norfolk, VA, April 2018).

6. M. A. Yarhouse, T. Morgan, D. Houp, and J. Sadusky, "Celibate Gay Christians: Sexual Identity and Religious Beliefs and Practices," *Journal of Pastoral Care and Counseling* 71.1 (2017): 52–59.

7. Yarhouse et al., "Pastors' Experiences."

Chapter 1: Church Culture Attitudes about LGBTQ+ Persons

1. We occasionally use the words *traditional* and *conservative* interchangeably to communicate the view that genital sexual intimacy is reserved for marriage between a man and a woman. We recognize, however, that being "conservative" on sexual ethics is different from being politically "conservative," and different again from other theological or social manifestations of conservatism.

2. C. Murphy, "Most U.S. Christian Groups Grow More Accepting of Homosexuality," Pew Research Center, December 18, 2015, www.pewresearch.org/fact-tank/2015/12/18/most-u-s-christian-groups-grow-more-accepting-of-homosexuality/.

3. Underlining original. It is interesting to note, however, that even these age-related changes may not tell the whole story: "At the same time, however, a larger segment of older adults in some Christian traditions have become accepting of homosexuality in recent years, helping to drive the broader trend. For instance, 32 percent of evangelical Protestant Baby Boomers now say homosexuality should be accepted, up from 25 percent in 2007" (Murphy, "U.S. Christian Groups").

4. M. A. Noll, D. W. Bebbington, and G. A. Rawlyk, *Evangelicalism* (New York: Oxford University Press, 1994), 6. Eastern Europe had its own movements.

5. The major components of evangelicalism include a recognition of the authority of the Bible, an emphasis on individual conversion or "new birth," an encouragement toward personal and community activism, and a faith in the redeeming work of Jesus Christ; see Noll, Bebbington, and Rawlyk, *Evangelicalism*.

6. R. V. Pierard argues that the "'evangelical spirit' has arisen throughout history and has been a part of the Apostolic church, the church fathers, early monasticism, medieval reform movements (Cluniac, Cistercian, Franciscan, and Dominican), preachers like Bernard of Clairvaux and Peter Waldo, the Brethren of the common life, and the Reformation precursors Wycliffe, Hus, and Savonarola" ("Evangelicalism," in W. A. Elwell, ed., *Evangelical Dictionary of Theology* [Grand Rapids: Baker, 1984], 380).

7. The Catechism states that this inclination is "intrinsically disordered" and is for most "a trial" (§2358). These wordings have been discussed at great length by celibate gay Christians and others. See *Catechism of the Catholic Church, with Modifications from the Editio Typica* (New York: Doubleday, 1994).

8. *Catechism of the Catholic Church.*

9. See "The Sides of the Divide," Bridges Across the Divide, http://web.archive.org/web/20100716091027/http://www.bridges-across.org/ba/sides.htm.

10. I. H. Meyer, "Minority Stress and Mental Health in Gay Men," National Center for Biotechnology Information (NCBI), March 1995, www.ncbi.nlm.nih.gov/pubmed/7738327.

11. D. M. Barnes and I. H. Meyer, "Religious Affiliation, Internalized Homophobia, and Mental Health in Lesbians, Gay Men, and Bisexuals," *American Journal of Orthopsychiatry* 82.4 (2012): 505–15.

12. The construct of internalized homophobia has been a point of some discussion among those who conduct research in this area. Internalized homophobia is sometimes measured by asking questions that some research subjects could answer affirmatively simply because of how their faith community understands sexuality and sexual behavior or how they themselves have come to understand these issues. (For example, an affirmative answer to the statement "You have wished that you could develop more feelings toward the opposite sex" could be taken as proof of internalized homophobia, or it could be regarded as a mark of a certain theological perspective.) Are these responses in and of themselves a reflection of internalized homophobia, or is it possible to pathologize people for adhering to a traditional Christian sexual ethic?

13. Barnes and Meyer, "Religious Affiliation," 513.

14. We recognize the inherent limitations in this sampling, especially after describing the range of theological difference even among those churches with a traditional Christian sexual ethic, both Protestant and Catholic. We do not make assumptions about the generalizability of these findings, but perhaps there are themes that can inform our broader discussion.

15. M. A. Yarhouse et al., "Pastors' Experiences with and Attitude toward Persons Who Experience Same-Sex Attraction in the Church," in *Understanding Sexuality: Perspectives and Challenges of the 21st Century*, ed. Oskar Enok and Jokum Rolf (New York: Nova Science, 2018), 49–78.

16. This is also (and not coincidentally) the title of Stanley Grenz's book, *Welcoming but Not Affirming* (Louisville: Westminster John Knox, 1998).

17. *Catechism of the Catholic Church*, 625–26.

18. Yarhouse et al., "Pastors' Experiences."

19. In a study we conducted on efforts to change sexual orientation through involvement in Christian ministries, we did find that, on average, people reported a shift along a continuum from attraction to the same sex to attraction to the opposite sex. However, averages mean more of a shift for some people and no shift for others. Also, given when the changes occurred (mostly from Time 1 to Time 2), there is reason to believe that what is most readily able to change is behavior and identity, though attractions may also change to some extent for some people. See our discussion of this in S. L. Jones and M. A. Yarhouse, "A Longitudinal Study of Attempted Religiously Mediated Sexual Orientation Change," *Journal of Sex and Marital Therapy* 37 (2011): 404–27.

20. This distinction is made in Yarhouse's prior work (M. A. Yarhouse, *Homosexuality and the Christian: A Guide for Parents, Pastors and Friends* [Minneapolis: Bethany, 2010], 158).

21. M. A. Yarhouse, T. Morgan, D. Houp, and J. Sadusky, "Celibate Gay Christians: Sexual Identity and Religious Beliefs and Practices," *Journal of Pastoral Care and Counseling* 71.1 (2017): 52–59.

22. M. A. Yarhouse, J. Dean, S. P. Stratton, and M. Lastoria, *Listening to Sexual Minorities: A Study of Faith and Sexual*

Identity on Christian College Campuses (Downers Grove, IL: IVP Academic, 2018).

23. We have changed the names of all our interviewees to protect their anonymity.

24. Melissa Steffan, "After Exodus: Evangelicals React as Ex-Gay Ministry Starts Over," *Christianity Today*, June 21, 2013, www.christianitytoday.com/ct/2013/june-web-only/exodus-international-alan-chambers-apologize-for-exgay-past.html.

25. Eve Tushnet, "The Botany Club: Gay Kids in Catholic Schools," The American Conservative, May 30, 2012, www.theamericanconservative.com/2012/05/30/the-botany-club-gay-kids-in-catholic-schools/.

26. Yarhouse et al., *Listening to Sexual Minorities*, 205–7, 288–93.

Chapter 2: LGBTQ+ Culture and the Church

1. Queer identity can be rather complicated. *Queer* is used differently by different people. Queer theory, derived from multiple sources, is critical of heteronormativity, which is the view that institutions value or privilege heterosexuality. Such a view attempts to deconstruct such assumptions and privilege because they reflect sources of oppression. To be queer can sometimes mean to reflect the idea that one pushes back against norms regarding heterosexuality.

2. This section is adapted from M. A. Yarhouse, J. Sides, and C. Page, "The Complexities of Multicultural Competence with LGBT+ Populations," in *Cultural Competence in Applied Psychology: Theory, Science, Practice, and Evaluation*, ed. Craig Frisby and William O'Donohue (New York: Springer, 2018).

3. Yarhouse, Sides, and Page, "Complexities."

4. "Persecution of Homosexuals in the Third Reich," United States Holocaust Memorial Museum, www.ushmm.org/wlc/en/article.php?ModuleId=10005261; Phil Davison, "Rudolf Brazda: Last Known Survivor of the 'Pink Triangle' Gay Inmates of Nazi Concentration Camps," *Independent*, August 9, 2011, www.independent.co.uk/news/obituaries/rudolf-brazda-last-known-survivor-of-the-pink-triangle-gay-inmates-of-nazi-concentration-camps-2334053.html.

5. E. M. Petchauer, M. A. Yarhouse, and L. Gallien, "Initiating a Culturally-Responsive Discourse of Same-Sex Attraction among

African-American Males," *Spaces for Difference: An Interdisciplinary Journal* 1.1 (2008): 1–17.

6. M. A. Fukuyama and A. D. Ferguson, "Lesbian, Gay, and Bisexual People of Color: Understanding Cultural Complexity and Managing Multiple Oppressions," in *Handbook of Counseling and Psychotherapy with Lesbian, Gay, and Bisexual Clients*, ed. R. M. Perez, K. A. DeBord, and K. J. Bieschke (Washington, DC: American Psychological Association, 2000), 99.

7. M. A. Yarhouse and J. N. Sells, *Family Therapies: A Comprehensive Christian Appraisal*, 2nd ed. (Downers Grove, IL: IVP Academic, 2017).

8. Jeffrey M. Jones, "In U.S., 10.2 percent of LGBT Adults Now Married to Same-Sex Spouse," Gallup, June 22, 2017, http://news.gallup.com/poll/212702/lgbt-adults-married-sex-spouse.aspx. When asked about their sexual identity, about 1.6 percent of US adults currently identify as gay or lesbian and 0.7 percent identify as bisexual (B. W. Ward, J. M. Dahlhamer, A. M. Galinsky, and S. S. Joestl, "Sexual Orientation and Health among US Adults: National Health Interview Survey, 2013," *National Health Statistics Report* 77 [July 15, 2014]: 1–10). A much smaller percentage have historically identified as transgender (ranging from 1 in 215 to 1 in 300; see K. J. Conron, G. Scott, G. S. Stowell, and S. J. Landers, "Transgender Health in Massachusetts: Results from a Household Probability Sample of Adults," *American Journal of Public Health* 102.1 [2012]: 118–22; G. J. Gates, "How Many People Are Gay, Bisexual, and Transgender?," Williams Institute, April 2011, http://williamsinstitute.law. ucla.edu/wp-content/uploads/Gates-How-Many-People-LGBT-Apr-2011.pdf), although this appears to be rising. *Transgender* is an umbrella term for many ways in which a person might identify or express or live out a gender identity differently than those whose biological sex (as male or female) and gender identity align. See Mark A. Yarhouse, *Understanding Gender Dysphoria: Navigating Transgender Issues in a Changing Culture* (Downers Grove, IL: IVP Academic, 2015).

9. It should be noted, too, that some of what is referred to as "lifestyle" may be related to discrimination insofar as societal views have affected how same-sex-oriented individuals meet one another, what they have seen modeled in terms of dating and

intimacy, and what expectations they bring to a relationship. In other words, societal views may have limited and shaped their opportunities to socialize and meet one another. More recent mainstreaming of LGBTQ+ persons and culture, it may be argued, has expanded such opportunities, as evidenced by the rise of internet dating, social networks, and religious faith communities that provide new avenues for meeting, dating, and socializing. See S. V. Giammattei and R. J. Green, "LGBTQ Couple and Family Therapy: History and Future Directions," in *Handbook of LGBT-Affirmative Couple and Family Therapy*, ed. J. Bigner and J. Wetchler (New York: Taylor & Francis, 2012), 1–22.

10. N. Gartrell, H. Bos, H. Peyser, A. Deck, and C. Rodas, "Family Characteristics, Custody Arrangements, and Adolescent Psychological Wellbeing after Lesbian Mothers Break Up," *Family Relations* 60 (2011): 572–85.

11. A. E. Goldberg and R. Garcia, "Predictors of Relationship Dissolution in Lesbian, Gay, and Heterosexual Adoptive Parents," *Journal of Family Psychology* 29.3 (2015): 394–404.

12. E. A. Carpenter-Song, M. A. Nordquest Schwallie, and J. Longhofer, "Cultural Competence Reexamined: Critique and Directions for the Future," *Psychiatric Services* 58 (2007): 1362.

13. M. A. Yarhouse, *Understanding Sexual Identity: A Resource for Youth Ministry* (Grand Rapids: Zondervan, 2013).

14. We are doubtful that there is one gay script today, especially about the relationship between sexuality and personhood, where there is significant disagreement in queer theory and activism, for instance, suggesting a multiplicity of scripts are at play.

15. Yarhouse, *Understanding Sexual Identity*, 70.

16. M. A. Yarhouse, J. Dean, S. P. Stratton, and M. Lastoria, *Listening to Sexual Minorities: A Study of Faith and Sexual Identity on Christian College Campuses* (Downers Grove, IL: IVP Academic, 2018).

17. See L. M. Diamond, *Sexual Fluidity: Understanding Women's Love and Desire* (Cambridge, MA: Harvard University Press, 2007).

18. Yarhouse, *Understanding Sexual Identity*, 70.

19. K. E. Maslowe and M. A. Yarhouse, "Christian Parental Reactions When a LGB Child Comes Out," *American Journal of Family Therapy* 43.4 (2015): 1–12.

20. M. Campbell, O. Zaporozhets, and M. A. Yarhouse, "Change in Parent-Child Relationships and Religious Views in Parents of LGB Youth Post-Disclosure," *Family Journal* (forthcoming).

Chapter 3: Experiences of Celibate Gay Christians

1. See "The Sides of the Divide," Bridges Across the Divide, http://web.archive.org/web/20100716091027/http://www.bridges-across.org/ba/sides.htm.
2. Rosaria Butterfield, "Grace to the City 2," Grace Presbyterian Church (Nashville), https://youtu.be/1_B7SmD1crU.
3. Mark Yarhouse, "Loneliness and the Celibate Gay Christian," *Spiritual Friendship* (blog), https://spiritualfriendship.org/2018/10/14/loneliness-and-the-celibate-gay-christian/.
4. Henri Nouwen, *Love, Henri: Letters on the Spiritual Life*, ed. Gabrielle Earnshaw (New York: Convergent, 2016), 188.
5. Nouwen, *Love, Henri*, 188–89.
6. Nouwen, *Love, Henri*, 189 (emphasis original).
7. That is, a standard deviation of sixteen years. High standard deviations indicate that data points are widely dispersed, whereas low standard deviations indicate that most of those surveyed were very close to the average value.
8. H. G. Koenig, K. G. Meador, and G. Parkerson, "Religion Index for Psychiatric Research," *American Journal of Psychiatry* 154 (1997): 885–86.
9. For a review of the research on etiology, see M. A. Yarhouse, *Homosexuality and the Christian: A Guide for Parents, Pastors and Friends* (Minneapolis: Bethany House, 2010).
10. A. W. R. Sipe, *A Secret World: Sexuality and the Search for Celibacy* (New York: Routledge, 1990).
11. Sipe, *Secret World*, 74.
12. See also A. W. R. Sipe, *Celibacy in Crisis: A Secret World Revisited* (New York: Routledge, 2003), 50.
13. Sipe, *Secret World*, 107; Sipe, *Celibacy in Crisis*, 50.
14. Sipe, *Secret World*, 139.
15. Sipe, *Secret World*, 147.
16. See, e.g., J. Loftus and R. Camarago, "Teaching the Clergy," *Annals of Sex Research* 6 (1993): 287–303.

17. E. Kennedy and V. Heckler, *The Catholic Priest in the United States* (Washington, DC: US Catholic Conference, 1972).

18. Kennedy and Heckler, *Catholic Priest*, 79.

19. S. Manuel, *Living Celibacy: Healthy Pathways for Priests* (Mahwah, NJ: Paulist, 2012), 16–17.

20. American Psychiatric Association, *Diagnostic and Statistical Manual of Mental Disorders*, 5th ed. (Arlington, VA: American Psychiatric Publishing, 2013).

21. B. D. Locke et al., "Development and Initial Validation of the Counseling Center Assessment of Psychological Symptoms-34 (CCAPS-34)," *Measurement and Evaluation in Counseling and Development* 45 (2012): 151–69.

22. R. A. Cummins et al., *Australian Unity Wellbeing Index: Cumulative Psychometric Record* (Melbourne: Australian Centre on Quality of Life, School of Psychology, Deakin University, 2004).

23. C. D. Ryff, "Happiness Is Everything, or Is It? Explorations on the Meaning of Psychological Well-Being," *Journal of Personality and Social Psychology* 57.6 (1989): 1069–81.

24. C. D. Ryff and C. L. M. Keyes, "The Structure of Psychological Well-Being Revisited," *Journal of Personality and Social Psychology* 69 (1995): 719–27.

25. M. A. Yarhouse, J. Dean, S. P. Stratton, and M. Lastoria, *Listening to Sexual Minorities: A Study of Faith and Sexual Identity on Christian College Campuses* (Downers Grove, IL: IVP Academic, 2018).

26. K. A. Brennan, C. L. Clark, P. R. Shaver, "Self-Report Measurement of Adult Attachment: An Integrative Overview," in *Attachment Theory and Close Relationships*, ed. J. A. Simpson and W. S. Rholes (New York: Guilford, 1998), 46–76.

27. C. Baker, O. Zaporozhets, M. A. Yarhouse, and M. Newmeyer, "Attachment, Well-Being, Distress, and Spirituality in Celibate Gay Christians" (paper presented at Southern Association for Counselor Education and Supervision 2016 Conference, New Orleans, LA, October 2016).

28. C. Baker, O. Zaporozhets, M. A. Yarhouse, and M. Newmeyer, "Attachment, Well-Being, Distress, and Spirituality in Celibate Gay Christians" (poster presented at American Counseling

Association National Conference, San Francisco, CA, March 2017).

29. Baker et al., "Attachment, Well-Being, Distress, and Spirituality" (paper); and Baker et al., "Attachment, Well-Being, Distress, and Spirituality in Celibate Gay Christians" (poster).

30. M. Mikulincer and P. R. Shaver, *Attachment in Adulthood: Structures, Dynamics, and Change*, 2nd ed. (New York: Guilford, 2016), 30.

31. Mikulincer and Shaver, *Attachment in Adulthood*, 30.

32. Mikulincer and Shaver, *Attachment in Adulthood*, 30–38.

33. K. D. Mickelson, R. C. Kessler, and P. R. Shaver, "Adult Attachment in a Nationally Representative Sample," *Journal of Personality and Social Psychology* 73.5 (1997): 1092–1106.

34. Mickelson, Kessler, and Shaver, "Adult Attachment," 1092–1106.

35. Thank you to Stephen P. Stratton for clarifying the dispositional versus interactional dimensions of attachment patterns.

Chapter 4: Celibate Gay Christians' Milestone Events

1. R. C. Savin-Williams and K. M. Cohen, "Homoerotic Development during Childhood and Adolescence," *Child and Adolescent Psychiatric Clinics of North America* 13 (2004): 540.

2. E. M. Dube and R. C. Savin-Williams, "Sexual Identity Development among Ethnic Sexual-Minority Male Youths," *Developmental Psychology* 35 (1999): 1389–99.

3. L. M. Diamond, *Sexual Fluidity: Understanding Women's Love and Desire* (Cambridge, MA: Harvard University Press, 2007); R. C. Savin-Williams, *The New Gay Teenager* (Cambridge, MA: Harvard University Press, 2006).

4. R. C. Savin-Williams and L. M. Diamond, "Sexual Identity Trajectories among Sexual-Minority Youths: Gender Comparisons," *Archives of Sexual Behavior* 29 (2000): 419–40.

5. M. A. Yarhouse and E. S. N. Tan, *Sexual Identity Synthesis: Attributions, Meaning-Making, and the Search for Congruence* (Lanham, MD: University Press of America, 2004).

6. M. A. Yarhouse, S. P. Stratton, J. B. Dean, and H. L. Brooke, "Listening to Sexual Minorities on Christian College Campuses," *Journal of Psychology and Theology* 37.2 (2009): 96–113.

7. S. P. Stratton, J. B. Dean, M. A. Yarhouse, and M. Lastoria, "Sexual Minorities in Faith-Based Education: A National Survey

of Attitudes, Milestones, Identity, and Religiosity," *Journal of Psychology and Theology* 41.1 (2013): 3–23.

8. M. A. Yarhouse, J. Dean, S. P. Stratton, and M. Lastoria, *Listening to Sexual Minorities: A Study of Faith and Sexual Identity on Christian College Campuses* (Downers Grove, IL: IVP Academic, 2018), 68, table 3.

9. Yarhouse et al., *Listening to Sexual Minorities*; see 68, table 3, and 133, table A4.3.

10. Diamond, *Sexual Fluidity*; Savin-Williams, *New Gay Teenager*.

11. M. Rosario, E. W. Schrimshaw, J. Hunter, and L. Braun, "Sexual Identity Development among Gay, Lesbian, and Bisexual Youths: Consistency and Change over Time," *Journal of Sex Research* 43.1 (2006): 46–58.

12. Yarhouse et al., *Listening to Sexual Minorities*.

13. Yarhouse et al., *Listening to Sexual Minorities*.

14. Yarhouse et al., *Listening to Sexual Minorities*, 68, table 3.1.

Chapter 5: Reflections for the Church

1. M. A. Yarhouse et al., "Pastors' Experiences with and Attitude toward Persons Who Experience Same-Sex Attraction in the Church," in *Understanding Sexuality: Perspectives and Challenges of the 21st Century*, ed. Oskar Enok and Jokum Rolf (New York: Nova Science, 2018).

2. Kyle Keating, "What Makes a Church Safe?" *Spiritual Friendship* (blog), https://spiritualfriendship.org/2013/09/16/what-makes-a-church-safe/.

3. Joseph Cardinal Ratzinger, "Letter to the Bishops of the Catholic Church on the Pastoral Care of Homosexual Persons," Congregation for the Doctrine of the Faith, October 1, 1986, www.vatican.va/roman_curia/congregations/cfaith/documents/rc_con_cfaith_doc_19861001_homosexual-persons_en.html.

4. Ron Belgau, "An Important Translation Issue," *Spiritual Friendship* (blog), https://spiritualfriendship.org/2018/01/05/an-important-translation-issue/#more-9441.

5. M. A. Yarhouse, J. Dean, S. P. Stratton, and M. Lastoria, *Listening to Sexual Minorities: A Study of Faith and Sexual Identity on Christian College Campuses* (Downers Grove, IL: IVP Academic, 2018).

6. Yarhouse et al., *Listening to Sexual Minorities*, 299.

7. M. Mikulincer and P. R. Shaver, *Attachment in Adulthood: Structures, Dynamics, and Change*, 2nd ed. (New York: Guilford, 2016).

8. Yarhouse et al., *Listening to Sexual Minorities*, 299.

9. Yarhouse et al., *Listening to Sexual Minorities*, 306.

10. Yarhouse et al., *Listening to Sexual Minorities*, 309.

Chapter 6: Celibate Gay Christians and Real Life

1. Wesley Hill, *Spiritual Friendship: Finding Love in the Church as a Celibate Gay Christian* (Grand Rapids: Brazos, 2015), 19–20.

2. Again, I would like to thank Stephen P. Stratton for his thoughts on an earlier draft of this manuscript and his reflections on church interactional patterns.

3. It may also be an indication that they already feel a degree of chemistry with the person they are inviting and that they sense the potential for a friendship to develop.

4. M. Mikulincer and P. R. Shaver, *Attachment in Adulthood: Structures, Dynamics, and Change*, 2nd ed. (New York: Guilford, 2016).

Chapter 7: How Celibate Gay Christians Could Strengthen the Church

1. Gregory Coles, *Single, Gay, Christian: A Personal Journey of Faith and Sexual Identity* (Downers Grove, IL: IVP, 2017), 38.

2. C. S. Lewis, cited in S. Vanauken, *A Severe Mercy* (New York: Harper & Row, 1977), 146–47.

3. C. S. Lewis, cited in Vanauken, *Severe Mercy*, 147–48.

4. M. A. Yarhouse, *Homosexuality and the Christian: A Resource for Parents, Pastors and Friends* (Minneapolis: Bethany House, 2010), 191, emphasis in original.

5. H. J. M. Nouwen, *Love, Henri: Letters on the Spiritual Life* (New York: Convergent, 2016), 192.

6. "Humility in Prosperity and Adversity," *Saintly Sages*, June 16, 2018, https://saintlysages.wordpress.com/2018/06/16/humility-in-prosperity-and-adversity-2/.

7. S. Pinckaers, *Morality: The Catholic View* (South Bend, IN: St. Augustine's Press, 2001), 78.

8. Pinckaers, *Morality*, 78.

9. Nouwen, *Love, Henri*, 137–38.
10. Wesley Hill, "The Ministry Gay Christians Have," *Spiritual Friendship* (blog), https://spiritualfriendship.org/2014/05/28/the-ministry-gay-christians-have/.

Conclusion

1. M. Mikulincer and P. R. Shaver, *Attachment in Adulthood: Structures, Dynamics, and Change*, 2nd ed. (New York: Guilford, 2016), 63.
2. Mikulincer and Shaver, *Attachment in Adulthood*, 63.
3. Mikulincer and Shaver, *Attachment in Adulthood*, 63.
4. Revoice, home page, http://www.revoice.us/.
5. http://revoice.us/PressReleases/June1PressRelease.pdf.
6. M. A. Yarhouse, *Understanding Sexual Identity* (Grand Rapids: Zondervan, 2013).